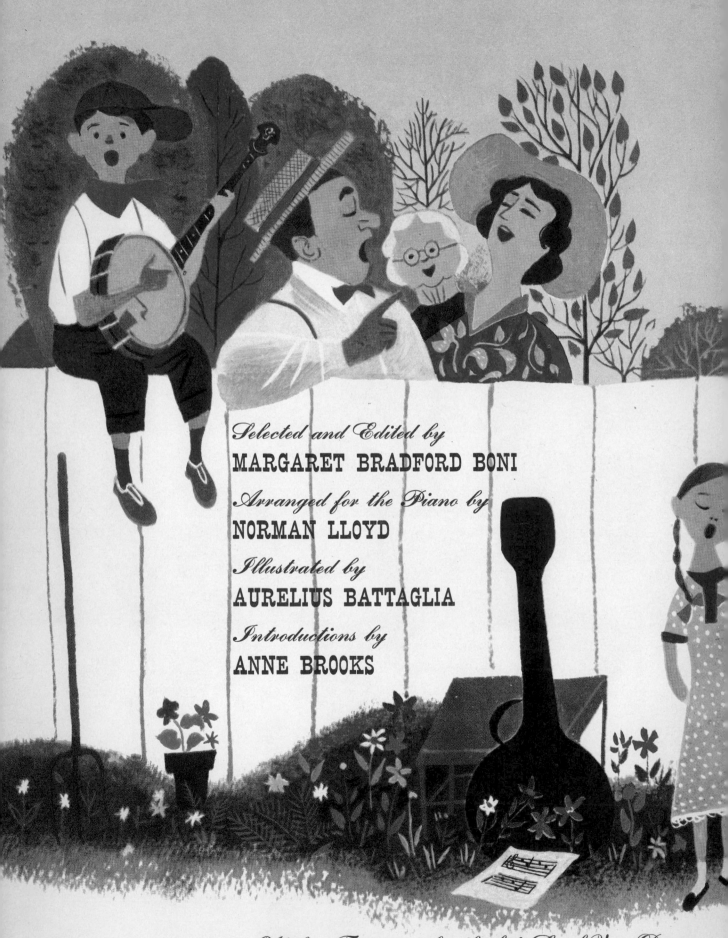

Selected and Edited by
MARGARET BRADFORD BONI
Arranged for the Piano by
NORMAN LLOYD
Illustrated by
AURELIUS BATTAGLIA
Introductions by
ANNE BROOKS

With a Foreword by the late Carl Van Doren

THE FIRESIDE BOOK
OF FAVORITE
AMERICAN SONGS

Simon and Schuster · New York

In Memory of
CARL VAN DOREN.

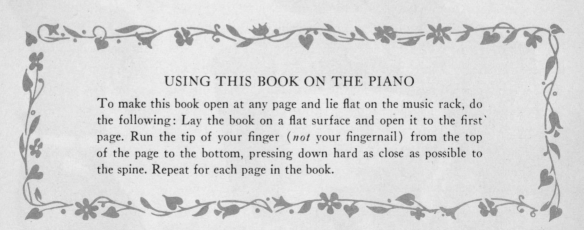

USING THIS BOOK ON THE PIANO

To make this book open at any page and lie flat on the music rack, do the following: Lay the book on a flat surface and open it to the first page. Run the tip of your finger (*not* your fingernail) from the top of the page to the bottom, pressing down hard as close as possible to the spine. Repeat for each page in the book.

FOREWORD

IT is at least sixty years since Nannie Coombes sang me a sad lullaby about Darling Nelly Gray, and I cried because, as I then misunderstood the story, some small boy had lost his mother and would never see her any more. The words and music still bring that experience hauntingly back to me. The words and music of dozens of songs in this book have now, as I turned through it, stirred up singing memories, of the time when I first heard a song, or of particular times—solemn, care-free, exultant, convivial—when I have joined in singing it with a few friends or with thousands of strangers united for the moment by the song.

Whoever opens this book will find himself at once at home in some room of his house of memory. Here, to begin with, are songs which filled the country half a century ago, when a gay decade abandoned itself to tearful ballads, and was martial for a year or so, and sentimental year after year, and yet sometimes tough and vernacular: all this in songs which outlived their first special vogues and settled into the general treasury of the nation's music.

Then there are songs of the half-century before that, concerned with slaves and slavery, and the soldiers of both armies in the Civil War, and the expanding nation with its canals, railroads, cowboys, mountaineers, and bandits. Before that again, songs of the Revolution and the fiery spirit of independence and the war with Mexico and the rush to California for gold. And at last, deeper down to the taproot of American life, to the days when America was still a colony not only of England but of the whole European world. The first settlers brought songs from France and Germany and the Netherlands, as well as from Scotland and Wales and Ireland. Their religion was reflected in their hymns, as were their traditional customs in their old ballads and rounds and songs for children.

It will seem surprising to most of us to find how many songs we now know well were sung so long ago. But a good song is timeless, a part of a nation like its constitution. It is a way we live. It is in our blood.

When an advance copy of THE FIRESIDE BOOK OF FOLK SONGS came to where I was visiting in the country, all the family and guests swarmed around the piano and began to sing. It went on for hours past midnight, and we found that more than ninety of the songs had been familiar enough to be sung without too much stumbling hesitation. Something like that, I am sure, will happen to THE FIRESIDE BOOK OF FAVORITE AMERICAN SONGS. They can be sung in any order, for study or for fun. Yet the chronological arrangement of the songs in each period sets them in a true perspective. Delightful as any one of these songs is in itself and by itself, history has made them, and they have made history. Whenever men, women, or children sing a nation's songs the singers are a part of the history of the nation.

CARL VAN DOREN

ACKNOWLEDGMENTS

I have consulted innumerable sources in compiling and editing this book, and should like to list them all. Since space is limited, however, I mention only the following, which I have found particularly useful: George Pullen Jackson's *White and Negro Spirituals, Down-East Spirituals and Others,* and *White Spirituals in the Southern Uplands;* John Tasker Howard's *Our American Music;* Henry Wilder Foote's *Three Centuries of American Hymnody;* Douglas Gilbert's *Lost Chords;* Isaac Goldberg's *Tin Pan Alley;* "Series of Old American Songs" from *The Harris Collection of American Poetry and Plays* with annotations by S. Foster Damon; Edward B. Marks' *They All Sang;* Sigmund Spaeth's *A History of Popular Music in America;* and *A Treasury of the Blues* by W. C.

Handy and Abbe Niles. I should like to express my appreciation to Miss Gladys Chamberlain of the Fifty-eighth Street Music Library, New York City, and to Dr. John Tasker Howard, Director of the Americana Section of the New York Public Library, for the many courtesies extended me in the preparation of this book. And I wish to thank Herbert Marks not only for allowing me to use important songs of the 90's and turn of the century, but for the generous amount of time he spent in discussing the background of the songs and of the periods in which they appeared. I remember gratefully, also, the late Carl Van Doren's enthusiastic response to the song material and the many helpful suggestions he gave.

MARGARET BONI

CONTENTS

II. CONFLICT AND EXPANSION: FROM 1850

III. INDEPENDENCE — ON TO THE WEST: FROM 1776

IV. THE PROMISED LAND: BEFORE 1776

Only Yesterday

FROM 1890

THE 1890's in America were years of lushness. The Industrial Revolution, which had got under way well before the Civil War, was now in full swing. While Andrew Carnegie, the Morgans, and later Rockefeller were carving fantastic fortunes in steel, finance, and oil, millions of other Americans caught the spirit of money making and dreamed of their own possible success. It was a time, as Andrew Carnegie himself described it, of "triumphant democracy."

During these years American music became fully commercialized. The days of the penny broadsheet and the street-corner peddler were gone. Large firms replaced the peddlers and gave nation-wide circulation to the songs of dozens of industrious writers. Charles K. Harris, one of the most popular song writers of the '90's, is credited with being the first of these publishers. He set up an office in Milwaukee and hung out a sign to advertise his wares. It read:

CHARLES K. HARRIS

Banjoist and Song Writer

Songs Written to Order

This was the tiny beginning of the great sprawling octopus of the music business which became known as New York's Tin Pan Alley.

Harris' own songs were typical of the lachrymose ballads which people at the end of the century loved. We still sing his "After the Ball," although few of us remember its ludicrous theme. His baby songs, "Hello Central, Give Me Heaven," "Baby

Hands," "For Sale, a Baby," and the others all tell stories calculated to wring the heart and are only slightly more naive than the other songs in vogue at the time, such as "A Little Lost Child," "Take Back Your Gold," and "Mother Was a Lady." It was the day of the great industrial expansion, and Americans, prosperous and relaxed, responded readily to the tear-jerkers Tin Pan Alley provided. As more and more musicians realized that song writing was a profitable profession, they produced a greater and greater number of sentimental songs.

In the same easy-going, unquestioning way, America was caught up in the world scramble for colonies. Our expanding production caused us to look for world markets. There was still much to be exploited in this country, but there was an emotional need for adventure which led many people to take up the "white man's burden." When the "Maine" was blown up in Havana Harbor and war was declared against Spain, our soldiers marched with two old songs dug up for the occasion. They weren't particularly martial, but it was not a particularly martial war. While the correspondents and the heroes were coining slogans—"You May Fire When You Are Ready, Gridley," "Don't Cheer, Boys: the Poor Fellows Are Dying," and other such noble sentiments—the soldiers were singing "Break the News to Mother" and "A Hot Time in the Old Town Tonight." The latter song was so popular that one French newspaper called it the American national anthem—"Il Fera Chaud dans la Vieille Ville ce Soir." Both of these songs had been written earlier—the hero of "Break the News to Mother" was originally a young fireman. But Tin Pan Alley gave them wholeheartedly to the soldiers of the most half-hearted war of our history.

Underneath the surface of this easy era, however, our social life was changing. The panic of 1893 had left its mark on the nation. The great industrialists were riding high, but there was labor unrest throughout the country. The working man began to demand his rights. There were great strikes—the McCormick Harvester Works strike which led to the Haymarket riots, the Pullman strike, the Cripple Creek War in Colorado, and the notorious Homestead strike. What is more, popular feeling sympathized with labor. One singer, J. W. Kelly, who called himself the "Rolling Mill Man," wrote a number of labor songs and won great popularity by them. His song about the Homestead strike cried out against "a grasping corporation" which had the audacity to demand, "You must all renounce your unions and forswear your liberty." And his chorus praised

> *"The man that fights for honor, none can blame him;*
> *May luck attend wherever he may roam;*
> *And no song of his will ever live to shame him*
> *While liberty and honor rule his home."*

Another, more singable song, written by William W. Delaney, cried:

> *"God help them tonight in their hour of affliction,*
> *Praying for him whom they'll ne'er see again.*
> *Hear the poor orphans tell their sad story,*
> *Father was killed by the Pinkerton men."*

Not only was the working man questioning the social status in those days. Reform was sweeping the church pulpits, and ministers were inveighing against Tammany, against corruption, against a newer, seemingly more lax way of living. The Salvation Army launched a great reform drive accompanied by a new series of songs designed to bring back the straying to the flock. Most of them were based on other popular songs of the day, some of them so solemnly that the Army failed to see how ludicrous they were. A popular Salvation Army ditty of the period, for instance, opened: "There are no flies on Jesus." However, others like "The Roll Is Called up Yonder" had a less preposterous effect and appealed to many who thought the nation was going to perdition.

In politics, Theodore Roosevelt was preparing to shake the big stick at monopolies and trusts, and the moral feeling of the times produced such individual reformers as Jacob Riis, who tried to clean up housing abuses, and later, statesmen like Robert M. LaFollette, who attempted to write reform into state and Federal laws.

The whole sentimental atmosphere of the '80's and early '90's was changing, and nothing shows it more clearly than the songs people were singing. The heroines of our newer songs had a roguish twinkle in their eyes, and such English music-hall importations as "You Don't Have to Marry the Girl" were in vogue. Some of the song writers

were still singing about babies and mothers and wronged girls, but others were parodying them. For instance, one successful ballad of the day was called "Just About to Fall." It asked that a helping hand be extended to the young man or woman about to succumb to temptation. A parody of the time was given the same title. But it tells the tale of a bloomer girl riding on a bicycle, who suddenly grips her bloomers with a look of horror, "For they're just about to fall."

Changing modes were bringing a spirit of restlessness to American society. People no longer stayed at home and sang around their pianos. It was the day of Trilby and bicycles. Nelly Bly raced around the world. The wealthy went to Europe; the less well-to-do organized trolley-car parties to the beaches, went to beer parlors and to theatres. Tony Pastor in New York made his theatre acceptable to ladies. He promised that there would be no smoking or drinking in the audience, and nothing offensive would take place on the stage. He offered door prizes of half barrels of flour, half tons of coal, dress patterns. The ladies were curious—they came—and they stayed. And with their advent, the pattern of entertainment began to change.

The minstrel show, which had been our earlier entertainment, had already been succeeded by whiteface performances. Now the core of the minstrel show, the "olio" or variety section, turned into vaudeville. Vaudeville in its place gave way to musical comedy with its sweet plots and sweet songs. "Daisy Bell," "Sweet Rosie O'Grady," and other songs of that kind were sung on the stages and whistled on the streets.

But along with the change in America's social life came a new type of music—ragtime. Nothing could have been more different in spirit than ragtime and the sentimental ballad. As one writer, Isaac Goldberg, says, "Babies disappeared; they gave way to 'babes' "!

Ragtime is a form of music which derives from the Negroes. The word itself comes from the Negro word for clog-dancing, which is "ragging." It means breaking up the rhythm of a song, syncopating it, giving it an irregular phrasing, probably best expressed in a song like Johnson and Cole's "Under the Bamboo Tree," which adds syllables to maintain its off-beat rhythm—"If you lak-a me like I lak-a you. . . ."

Like all the new forms of music which were to come into vogue, ragtime could be traced back to the irregular beat of the spirituals, the same element which Foster and Bland had picked up to some extent in their songs. But now, in its truer, rawer form, the syncopated beat became the all-absorbing passion of the nation. It appeared first as instrumental music, piano arrangements which were variations on such songs as "Mr. Johnson, Turn Me Loose" and "Oh, I Don't Know, You're Not So Warm." In short order, however, the ragtime song appeared; "My Gal's a Highborn Lady" is supposed to have been the first.

With the ragtime song came a form of art known as "coon-shouting," mostly performed by men, although a few women with appropriately husky voices were successful at it. The "cakewalk" typified by such songs as "At a Georgia Camp Meeting" was an allied art. All of these new types of music—the cakewalk, coon-shouting, and ragtime—were getting closer to the Negro folk song, which has so profoundly affected American music for the last century. But they were still written for the most part by white people, and they were still synthetic in comparison with the real jazz and the blues which were to follow.

Jazz and its variations, such as swing and be-bop, is music of today and is more typical of a recent period than it is of earlier days. But it had its beginnings at the turn of the century, and it was accepted by the nation then in its new and changing mood—the mood which was to bring about our participation in World War I, to emancipate our women, to give us the bob and the short skirt, the flapper and bootleg gin. These things were the ultimate expression of our changing sentiment. The mood and the music had earlier origins.

The beginnings of jazz were the blues. And if we can thank anybody for the popularization of the blues as we know them, it is W. C. Handy. Handy started as a band leader, by playing classical or semi-classical music, or the Broadway songs of Charles Harris, Paul Dresser, and the others. But he found they were not half so popular as the sad, discordant "blues" of his own people. These blues were sung by Negroes on street corners, by itinerant guitar players and barroom pianists, and they were already a part of the nation's folklore. Unlike the spirituals, they were not choral music—they were sung by one man and expressed one man's rueful tragedy. They were rife with barroom and street slang, but they had a vividness of expression which said far more than the pseudo-tearful ditties of Broadway. They were hypnotic and slurring, and their harmonies had the power to shock. When Handy wrote his first blues, the political song "Mister Crump," later to be known as "Memphis Blues," his fame and the popularity of that type of music were assured.

From blues to jazz was an easy step. The band players liked to improvise on the simple blues tunes, and in their syncopated variations were the seeds of jazz. Later, Broadway was to take it up, it was to spread to Europe, it was to influence the composers of classical music. A world war, a new generation, modern and freer social conventions were to make it acceptable to everybody. Today, jazz is a part of our daily life. At the turn of the century, it was an expression of change in a changing nation which was growing out of adolescence into a new maturity.

Daisy Bell

[A BICYCLE BUILT FOR TWO]

Harry Dacre, an English song writer, came to this country in the 90's. He brought his bicycle along with him and was astounded when the customs officials charged him duty on it. A chance remark of a friend, "Lucky for you it was not built for two," gave Dacre the idea for his famous bicycle song, "Daisy Bell," which started the whole cycle of bicycle songs so popular in the 90's.

Words and Music by Harry Dacre

1. There is a flow-er with-in my heart, Dai-sy, Dai—sy! Plant-ed one day by a
2. We will go "tan-dem" as man and wife, Dai-sy, Dai—sy! "Ped-dling" a-way down the

ford a car-riage,_____ But you'll look sweet

On the seat of a bi-cy-cle built for two!_____

3. I will stand by you in "wheel" or woe,
Daisy, Daisy!
You'll be the bell(e) which I'll ring, you know!
Sweet little Daisy Bell!
You'll take the "lead" in each "trip" we take,
Then, if I don't do well,
I will permit you to use the brake,
My beautiful Daisy Bell!

CHORUS

Daisy, Daisy,
Give me your answer, do!
I'm half crazy,
All for the love of you!
It won't be a stylish marriage,
I can't afford a carriage,
But you'll look sweet
On the seat
Of a bicycle built for two!

Ta-Ra-Ra-Boom-Der-E

"Ta-Ra-Ra-Boom-Der-E" was published in 1891. Henry Sayers, the composer, frankly says that the tune originated in Babe Conner's famous St. Louis brothel, sung by the fabulous Negro singer Mama Lou. Sayers' song was a complete failure: America would have nothing to do with it. A year later, Lottie Collins, well-known music-hall singer of the day, sang it in London. Overnight it became a sensation. The music-hall crowds delighted in its rollicking rhythm and its nonsensical, naughtyish lines. Brought back to America by Lottie Collins in 1894, it was greeted with the same wild enthusiasm that the English had accorded it, and has remained one of America's most popular songs.

Words and Music by Henry J. Sayers

1. A sweet Tux - e - do girl you see, Queen of swell so -
2. I'm a blush-ing bud of in - no-cence, Pa - pa says at

ci - e - ty, Fond of fun as fond can be,
big ex - pense, Old maids say I have no sense,

Mother Was a Lady

This seemingly imperishable ballad originated in the mid-90's in a little basement saloon on Twenty-first Street, New York. Edward Marks and Joseph Stern overheard two men teasing a new waitress, who finally burst into tears and said, "No one would dare to insult me if my brother Jack was only here," adding, "My mother was a lady." Marks, recognizing the possibilities of the line, immediately wrote the lyric and Stern supplied the music. The song was sung with great success the next day at Tony Pastor's theatre.

Words by Edward B. Marks

Music by Joseph W. Stern

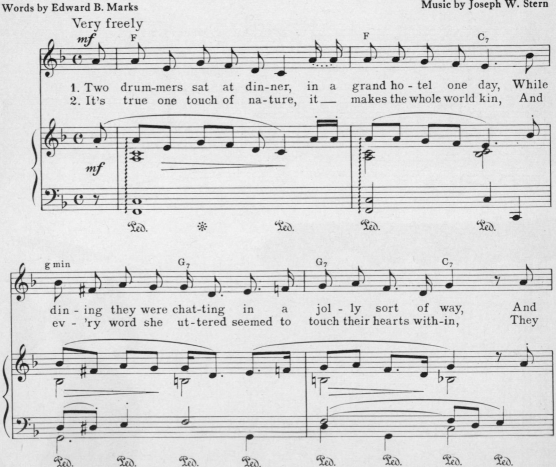

Very freely

1. Two drum-mers sat at din-ner, in a grand ho-tel one day, While
2. It's true one touch of na-ture, it_ makes the whole world kin, And

din - ing they were chat-ting in a jol - ly sort of way, And
ev - 'ry word she ut-tered seemed to touch their hearts with-in, They

There'll Be a Hot Time

The Spanish-American War turned to earlier eras for its songs.
"Hot Times," sung and played fully twelve years before, was
the favorite marching song of the soldiers, and is said to have
been adopted by Theodore Roosevelt as the official song of his
Rough Riders. The original lines of "Hot Times," as sung in
Babe Conner's brothel in St. Louis, years before, had nothing
to do with marching men. They told of a Negro
who had lost his love.

Words by Joe Hayden

Music by Theo. A. Metz

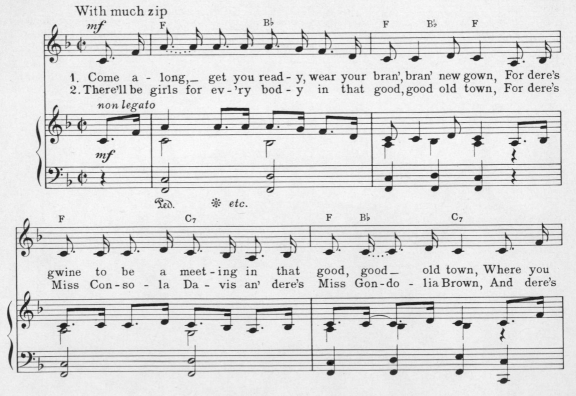

With much zip

1. Come a - long,— get you read - y, wear your bran', bran' new gown, For dere's
2. There'll be girls for ev - 'ry bod - y in that good, good old town, For dere's

gwine to be a meet - ing in that good, good— old town, Where you
Miss Con - so - la Da - vis an' dere's Miss Gon - do - lia Brown, And dere's

know - ded ev - 'ry - bod - y and dey all know - ded you And you've
Miss Jo - han - na Beas - ly, she am dressed all in red, I just

got a rab - bit's foot to keep a - way de hoo - doo.
hugged her and I kissed her and to me then she said:

When you hear that the preach - ing does be - gin.
"Please, oh, please, oh,— do not let me fall.

Bend down low for to drive a - way your sin, And when you
You're all mine and I love you best of all, And you must

gets re - li - gion you want to shout and sing, There'll be a
be my man or I'll have no man at all, There'll be a

hot time in the old town to - night, my ba - by.
hot time in the old town to - night, my ba - by."

Chorus

When you hear dem - a bells go ding, ling, ling,

Ped. ❋ Ped. ❋ etc.

After the Ball

This song, which became the leading sob ballad of the 90's, according to its author was based upon an actual incident. A young couple, engaged to be married, quarreled one evening at a ball. Harris saw the young girl, evidently in deep distress, depart alone for home. He quickly jotted down the line "Many a heart is aching after the ball." The next day, in an hour's time, the whole of "After the Ball" was written.

Allegro

Words and Music by Charles K. Harris

1. A lit - tle maid - en climbed an old man's knee, _____ Begged for a sto - ry, "Do,

2. "Bright lights were flash - ing in the grand ball- room, _____ Soft - ly the mu - sic, play -

pet, you will soon know. _____ List to the
heart, as lov - ers can. _____ Down fell the

sto - ry, I'll tell it all, _____ I be-
glass, pet, bro - ken, that's all, _____ Just _____

liev'd her faith - less, af - ter the ball." _____
as my heart was, af - ter the ball." _____

3. Long years have passed, child. I've never wed,
True to my lost love, though she is dead.
She tried to tell me, tried to explain;
I would not listen, pleadings were vain.
One day a letter came from that man;
He was her brother, the letter ran.
That's why I'm lonely, no home at all;
I broke her heart, pet, after the ball.

CHORUS

After the ball is over,
After the break of morn,
After the dancers' leaving,
After the stars are gone;
Many a heart is aching,
If you could read them all;
Many the hopes that have vanish'd
After the ball.

Break the News to Mother

*A sentimental ballad of earlier years, made popular
by the Spanish-American War.*

Words and Music by Charles K. Harris

Freely—not too slowly

1. While the shot and shell were scream-ing up-on the bat-tle-field; The
2. From a-far a not-ed gen-'ral had wit-nessed his brave deed. "Who

boys in blue were fight-ing their no-ble flag to shield; Came a
saved our flag? Speak up, lads; 'twas no-ble, brave in-deed!" "There he

flag but gave his young life; all for his coun-try's sake. They
son, my brave young he - ro; I thought you safe at home." "For-

poco rit.

brought him back and soft - ly heard him say:
give me, Fa - ther, for I ran a - way."

Chorus
mp a tempo

"Just break the news to Moth-er; She knows how dear I love her, And

tell her not to wait for me, For I'm not com - ing home; Just

At a Georgia Camp Meeting

The cakewalk, an eccentric, strutting dance, was the sensation of the mid-90's. And Kerry Mills' song, forerunner of the two-step and fox trot, was the greatest cakewalk tune of the time.

Words and Music by Kerry Mills

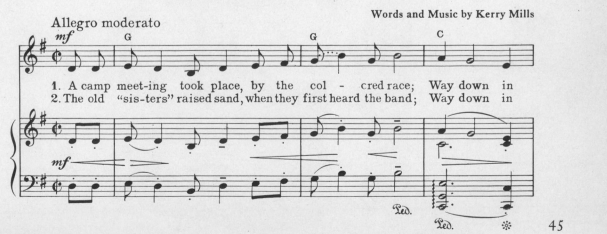

Allegro moderato

1. A camp meet-ing took place, by the col - ored race; Way down in
2. The old "sis-ters" raised sand, when they first heard the band; Way down in

The Little Lost Child

*Child songs were in great demand during the middle
90's, and this "heart" story of the lost child, with its
happy ending and ingratiating tune, became
one of the big hits of the day.*

Words by Edward B. Marks

Music by Joseph W. Stern

1. A pass - ing po - lice - man found a lit - tle child,
2. "'Twas all through a quar - rel, mad - ly jeal - ous she,

She walked be - side him, dried her tears and smiled.
Vowed then to leave me, wom - an - like, you see.

Said he   to her kind - ly,   "Now you must not cry, ___
___ Oh,   how I loved her;   grief near drove me wild." ___

I will find your ma - ma   for   you bye and   bye." ___
"Pa - pa, you are cry - ing;" lisped the lit - tle child. ___

At   the sta - tion when   he ___ asked her for her name, ___
Sud - den - ly   the door   of the sta - tion o - pened wide, ___

And she an - swered, "Jen - nie." ___ It made him ex - claim: ___   "At
"Have you seen   my dar - ling?" An anx - ious moth - er cried. ___

49

last of your moth - er I have now a trace;___
Hus - band and wife then meet - ing face to face;___

Your__ lit - tle fea - tures bring back her sweet face."___
All is soon for - giv - en, in one fond em - brace.___

Chorus

"Do not fear my lit - tle dar - ling, And { I will take you right home.___
(2nd) { we

Come and sit down close be - side { me, No more from { me you shall roam.___ For
{ us, { us

you were a babe in arms When your moth-er left me one day,___

Left me at home, de-sert-ed, a - lone, And took you, my child, a - way."___

She Was Bred in Old Kentucky

A charming song of 1898.

Words by Harry Braisted

Music by Stanley Carter

1. When a lad, I stood one day by a
2. Man-y years have passed a-way since that

cot-tage far a-way, And to me that day, all na-ture seem'd more
well re-mem-ber'd day, When to that dear old Ken-tuck-y home I

grand;_____ For my Sue, with blush-es red, had just
came;_____ And my hap-pi-ness thro' life, was my

She Was Bred in Old Kentucky

54

face and man - ner, too, She was bred in old Ken-tuck-y, Take her,

boy, you're might-y luck-y, When you mar-ry a girl like Sue."

It's the Syme the Whole World Over

The lyrics of this popular satire, Carl Sandburg says, were fortified in part by H. L. Mencken and a contributor to The American Mercury.

With a throb

1. It's the syme the whole world o-ver,_____ 'Tis the poor what
2. She_ was a par-son's daugh-ter,_____ Pure,un-styn-ed

gets the blyme,_____ While the rich 'as all the
was her fyme,_____ Till a coun-try squire came

ply-sures._____ Now_ ain't that a blink-in' shyme?_____
court-in', And the poor_ girl lost her nyme._____

3. So she went aw'y to Lunnon,
   Just to 'ide her guilty shyme.
   There she met an Army Chaplain:
   Ornst ag'yn she lorst her nyme.

4. 'Ear 'im as he jaws the Tommies,
   Warnin' o' the flymes o' 'ell.
   With 'er 'ole 'eart she had trusted,
   But ag'yn she lorst her nyme.

5. Now 'e's in his ridin' britches,
   'Untin' foxes in the chyse
   W'ile the wictim o' his folly
   Makes her livin' by her wice.

6. So she settled down in Lunnon,
   Sinkin' deeper in her shyme,
   Till she met a lybor leader,
   And ag'yn she lorst 'er nyme.

7. Now 'e's in the 'Ouse o' Commons,
   Mykin' laws to put down crime,
   W'ile the wictim of his plysure
   Walks the street each night in shyme.

8. Then there cyme a bloated bishop.
   Marriage was the tyle 'e tole.
   There was no one else to tyke 'er,
   So she sold 'er soul for gold.

9. See 'er in 'er 'orse and carriage,
   Drivin' d'ily through the park.
   Though she's myde a wealthy marriage
   Still she 'ides a brykin' 'eart.

10. In a cottage down in Sussex
    Lives 'er parents old and lyme,
    And they drink the wine she sends 'em,
    But they never, never, speaks 'er nyme.

11. In their poor and 'umble dwellin'
    There 'er grievin' payrents live,
    Drinkin' champyne as she sends 'em,
    But they never, never, can forgive.

12. It's the syme the whole world over,
    It's the poor what gets the blyme,
    While the rich 'as all the plysures.
    Now ayn't it a bloody shyme?

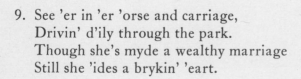

Take Back Your Gold

Monroe Rosenfeld, described by Edward Marks as "a melodic kleptomaniac," wrote songs filled with the sentiment and moralities pleasing to his times. "Take Back Your Gold," pleading that happiness can never be purchased, achieved tremendous popularity. Rosenfeld is generally credited with having invented the name Tin Pan Alley.

Words by Louis W. Pritzkow

Music by Monroe H. Rosenfeld

1. I saw a youth and maid-en on a lone-ly cit-y street, And thought them lov-ers at their meet-ing place, _____ Un -
2. He drew her close un-to him and to soothe her then he tried, But she in pride and sor-row turned a-way, _____ And

when he said,"You shall not want, what - ev - er may be - fall" She
gold will help you to for - get?" But with a break-ing heart, She

Broadly

spurned the gold he of - fered her and said:
scorned his gift and bit - ter - ly re - plied:

Chorus
stoutly

"Take back your gold, for gold can nev - er buy me;

Take back your bribe, and prom-ise you'll be true; Give me the love, - the

love that you'd de-ny me; Make me your wife, that's all I ask of you."

Oh Promise Me

Reginald De Koven's famous song of 1889 appears in "Robin Hood," one of the most successful of American comic operas. It is still a favorite song, and today has become an essential part of all conventional wedding services.

Words by Clement Scott

Music by Reginald De Koven

1. Oh, prom-ise me that some day you and I
Will take our love to-geth-er to some sky
new, And find the hol-lows where those flow-ers grew, Those

prom-ise me that you will take my hand,
The most un-wor-thy in this lone-ly land,
eyes, See - ing the vi - sion of our par - a-dise,

Where we can be a-lone, and faith re-new,
And let me sit be-side you, in your

Frankie and Johnnie

"If America has a classical gutter song," says Carl Sandburg, *"it is this one that tells of Frankie and her man."* This sordid tale of two lovers has been sung in versions by the hundreds throughout the country, possibly since the late 70's. Abbe Niles, an authority on the "blues," claims to know nearly 500 versions. The complete melody of *"Frankie and Johnnie,"* according to Sigmund Spaeth, was not published until 1912.

1. Frank-ie and John-nie were lov-ers!
2. Frank-ie went down to the cor-ner,

Oh, Lord-y, how they could love! They swore to be true to each
Just for a buck-et of beer. She said to the fat bar-

Frankie and Johnnie

oth - er,   Just as   true_ as the stars   a - bove,_   He   was   her
ten - der,   "Has my   lov - in - est_ man been here?_   He   was   my

3. "I don't want to cause you no trouble, I don't want to tell you no lie;
   But I saw your man an hour ago with a gal named Alice Bly,
   And if he's your man, he's a-doin' you wrong."

4. Frankie went down to the pawnshop; she bought herself a little forty-four.
   She aimed it at the ceiling, shot a big hole in the floor.
   "Where is my man? He's doin' me wrong."

5. Frankie went down to the hotel; she rang the hotel bell.
   "Get out of my way, all you floozies, or I'll blow you straight to hell.
   I want my man who is doin' me wrong."

6. Frankie looked over the transom, and found, to her great surprise,
   That there in the room sat Johnnie a-lovin' up Alice Bly.
   He was her man but he done her wrong.

7. Frankie threw back her kimono, she took out her little forty-four.
   Root-a-toot, three times she shot, right through that hardwood floor.
   She shot her man 'cause he done her wrong.

man,_____ But he done her wrong. _____
man,_____ But he's done me wrong."_____

8. Johnnie he grabbed off his Stetson, "O good Lawd, Frankie, don't shoot!"
But Frankie put her finger on the trigger and the gun went roota-toot-toot.
He was her man but she shot him down.

9. "Roll me over easy, roll me over slow;
Roll me over easy, boys, 'cause my wounds they hurt me so.
I was your man but I done you wrong."

10. "Oh, bring on your rubber-tired hearses, oh, bring on your rubber-tired hacks.
They're taking your man to the graveyard and they ain't goin' to bring him back.
He was your man but he done you wrong."

11. "Oh, bring 'round a thousand policemen, bring 'em around today,
To lock me in that dungeon and throw the key away.
I shot my man 'cause he done me wrong."

12. This story has no moral, this story has no end.
This story only goes to show that there ain't no good in men.
They'll do you wrong just as sure as you're born.

Under the Bamboo Tree

One day Bob Cole heard Rosamond Johnson humming "No-body Knows de Trouble I See," and suddenly recognized the possibilities in the syncopated chorus for the ragtime piece they so badly needed for their show. Johnson was finally persuaded; and the fine old chorus, with a simple inversion of its melodic line and words worked out by Cole, became the chorus of "Under the Bamboo Tree," the top song of the Cole and Johnson partnership.

Words by Bob Cole

Music by Rosamond Johnson

1. Down in the jun-gles lived a maid,— Of roy-al blood though dusk-y shade,— A marked im-pres-sion once she made—
2. And in this sim-ple jun-gle way,— He wooed the maid-en ev-'ry day, By sing-ing what he had to say;—

Up-on a Zu-lu from Ma-ta-boo-loo; And ev-'ry morn-ing
One day he seized her and gen-tly squeezed her; And there be-neath the

he would be___ Down un-der-neath a bam-boo tree,___
bam-boo green,___ He begged her to be-come his queen;___

A-wait-ing there his love to see___ And then to her he'd sing:___
The dusk-y maid-en blushed un-seen___ And joined him in his song.___

Not too fast

If you lak-a-me, lak I lak-a-you, And we lak-a both the

same, I lak-a say, this ver-y day, I lak-a change your

name;— 'Cause I love-a-you and love-a-you true And if you-a love-a me,

One live as two,   two live as one   Un-der the bam-boo tree.   If   tree.

3. This little story, strange but true,
   Is often told in Mataboo,
   Of how this Zulu tried to woo
   His jungle lady in tropics shady.
   Although the scene was miles away,
   Right here at home, I dare to say,
   You'll hear some Zulu ev'ry day
   Gush out this soft refrain:

   CHORUS
   If you laka me, lak I laka you;
   And we laka both the same,
   I laka say, this very day,
   I laka change your name;
   'Cause I love-a you and love-a you true
   And if you-a love-a me,
   One live as two, two live as one
   Under the bamboo tree.

71

Glow Worm

(GLÜHWÜRMCHEN)

In the late 90's Paul Lincke's "Glühwürmchen" was introduced in Lew Field's "The Girl Behind the Counter" and became the song hit of that show. Later Anna Pavlova used the tune for her "Empire Gavotte." It is now considered one of the classics of popular music—a favorite number of small orchestras, and an ever-popular piano solo.

Words by Lilla Cayley Robinson

Music by Paul Lincke

1.When the night falls si - lent - ly,— the night falls si - lent - ly— on for-ests
2."Lit - tle glow-worm, tell me pray,— oh, glow-worm, tell me pray,— how did you

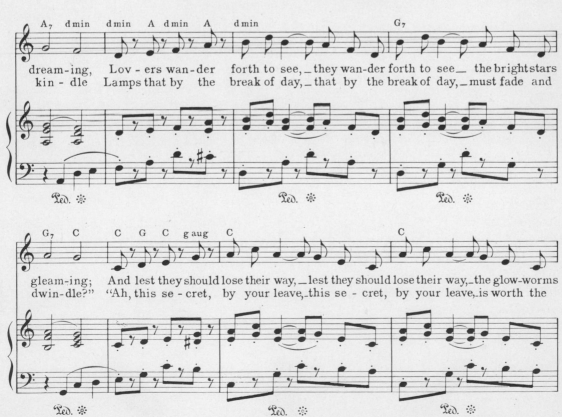

dream-ing, Lov-ers wan-der forth to see,— they wan-der forth to see— the bright stars
kin-dle Lamps that by the break of day,— that by the break of day,— must fade and

gleam-ing; And lest they should lose their way,— lest they should lose their way,— the glow-worms
dwin-dle?" "Ah, this se-cret, by your leave,— this se-cret, by your leave, is worth the

night - ly Light their ti - ny lan-terns gay,_their ti - ny lan-terns gay,_ and twin-kle
learn - ing! When true lov-ers come at eve,_true lov-ers come at eve,_their hearts are

bright-ly. Here and there, and ev-'ry-where, from moss-y dell and hol-low,
burn - ing! Glow-ing cheeks and lips be-tray, how sweet the kiss-es tast-ed!

Float-ing, glid-ing through the air, they call on us to fol - low!
Till we steal the fire a-way, for fear lest it be wast - ed!"

74

75

In the Good Old Summertime

"There's nothing like the good old summertime," said George Evans one evening to Ren Shields. And this suggested the title of one of the big song hits of 1902. It is hardly less popular now than then.

Words by Ren Shields

Music by George Evans

hold her hand and she holds yours, and that's a ver - y good sign___ That she's your toot - sey woot - sey in the good old sum - mer time.___

Ballet of the Boll Weevil

It was late in the 90's when the boll weevil crossed the Rio Grande into Texas. Since then every cotton-growing state has been invaded by these destructive black bugs, and each state has sung its own version of the depredation wrought by them.

Words and Melody adapted and arranged by John A. and Alan Lomax

1. O have you heard de lat - es',____ De lat - es' of de songs? It's a - bout dem lit - tle boll

2. De boll wee - vil is a lit - tle black bug F'um Mex - i - co, dey say, He___ come to try___ dis

wee - vils Picked up bofe feet an' gone,} A - look-in' for a
Tex-as soil An' thought he'd bet-ter stay,

home,_____ Jes' a-look-in' for a home, A - look-in' for a

home,_____ Jes' a-look-in' for a home._____

3. De fus' time I seen de boll weevil
   He was settin' on de square;
   De nex' time I saw de boll weevil
   He had all his family dere—

   CHORUS
   Dey's lookin' for a home,
   Jes' a-lookin' for a home,
   Dey's lookin' for a home,
   Jes' a-lookin' for a home.

4. De third time I seen de boll weevil
   He was on the western plain;
   Nex' time I seen de boll weevil,
   He had hopped dat Memphis train,

   CHORUS
   Lookin' for a home,
   Jes' a-lookin' for a home,
   Lookin' for a home,
   Jes' a-lookin' for a home.

5. De farmer took de boll weevil
   An' buried him in hot sand;
   De boll weevil say to de farmer,
   "I'll stand it like a man,

   CHORUS
   "For it is my home,
   It is my home,
   For it is my home,
   It is my home."

6. Den de farmer took de boll weevil
   An' lef' him on de ice;
   De boll weevil say to de farmer,
   "Dis is mighty cool an' nice.

   CHORUS
   "O it is-a my home,
   It is my home,
   O it is-a my home,
   It is my home."

7. Mr. Farmer took little weevil
   An' fed him on Paris Green;
   "Thank you, Mr. Farmer,
   It's the best I ever seen.

   CHORUS
   "It is my home,
   It's jes' my home,
   It is my home,
   It's jes' my home."

8. De boll weevil say to de farmer,
   "You better lemme 'lone,
   I et up all yo' cotton,
   An' now I'll begin on de co'n.

   CHORUS
   "I'll have a home,
   I'll have a home,
   I'll have a home,
   I'll have a home."

9. De merchant got half de cotton,
   De boll weevil got de rest;
   Didn't leave de po' ol' farmer
   But one old cotton dress;

   CHORUS
   An' it's full o' holes,
   O, it's full o' holes,
   An' it's full o' holes,
   O, it's full o' holes.

10. De farmer say to de merchant,
    "I ain't made but one bale,
    But befo' I'll give you dat one
    I'll fight an' go to jail.

    CHORUS
    "I'll have a home,
    I'll have a home,
    I'll have a home,
    I'll have a home."

11. Ef anybody axes you
    Who wuz it writ dis song,
    Tell 'em 'twas a dark-skinned farmer
    Wid a pair o' blue duckin's on,

    CHORUS
    A-lookin' for a home,
    Jes' a-lookin' for a home,
    A-lookin' for a home,
    Jes' a-lookin' for a home.

Lazy Moon

*An outstanding song of the year 1903,
and an interesting example of the
ballad fox-trot rhythm.*

Words by Bob Cole

Music by Rosamond Johnson

1. La - zy moon! come out soon!
2. Though it's late, still I wait,

Make my— poor heart beat warm-er;
Watch-ing— for her and pin - ing;

Light the way! bright as day,
But a cloud, like a shroud,

84

For my ___ sweet lit - tle charm-er; She's to meet me in the
Keeps the ___ old moon from shin-ing; If I do not see my

lane to-night, If the sky is bright and clear; ___
queen to-night, Still I know her heart is true; ___

Moon! don't make me wait in vain to-night, Watch-ing and a - wait - ing,
'Tis be-cause the moon is mean to-night, Hid - ing and a - creep-ing,

Lazy Moon

Heart a - pal - pi - tat - ing, Long-ing for my la - dy love so dear.____
Will not come a - peep-ing, Now I won-der what I'm going to do.____

Chorus
a tempo

La - zy moon! la - zy moon! Why

don't you show your face a - bove the hill?____ La - zy moon!

come____ out soon! You can make me hap - py if you will;____

When my la - dy sees your face a - peep-ing,

Then I know her prom-ise she'll be keep-ing; Tell__ me, what's__ the

mat - ter, are you sleep-ing?__ La - zy moon._____

Bill Bailey, Won't You Please Come Home?

A popular ragtime song of 1902.

Words and Music by Hughie Cannon

"Won't you come home, Bill Bai-ley, won't you come home?" She moans the

whole day long, _____ "I'll do de cook-ing, dar-ling,

88

Midnight Special

Many legends are connected with this jail song. One, told by Pete Seeger, is the belief among some of the prisoners that if the light from the midnight special, as it passed the prison, should fall on a man sleeping in his cell, that man would go free.

1. Well, you wake up in the morn - ing,_____
2. If you go_ to_ Hous - ton,_____

_____ Hear the ding-dong ring,_____ You go a-march-ing to the
_____ You_ bet-ter walk right,_____ You_ bet - ter not_

90

From *Our Singing Country*, compiled and copyrighted by John A. and Alan Lomax.

Midnight Special

Shine her ev - er - lov - ing light on me.

3. Yonder comes Miss Rosie,
How'n the world do you know?
Well, I know her by her apron
And the dress she wore;
Umbrella on her shoulder,
Piece of paper in her hand,
Goes a-marching to the captain,
Says, "I want my man."

4. I'm going away to leave you,
And my time ain't long;
The man is going to call me,
And I'm going home;
Then I'll be done my grieving,
Whooping, hollering, and crying,
I'll be done my studying
About my great long time.

CHORUS

Let the midnight special
Shine her light on me;
Let the midnight special
Shine her ever-loving light on me.

Ida, Sweet as Apple Cider

A favorite song of 1903, and a pleasing example of the song type
popular in the new century. Ballads of fallen girls and kept women,
set to the monotonous "dum-dum-diddle" style of accompaniment,
were no longer acceptable. Song writers, to be popular,
had now to supply songs with a more moral content,
set to a good melody and lilting rhythm.

Lyric by Eddie Leonard   Music by Eddie Munson

1. In the re - gion where the ros - es al - ways bloom,_____
2. When the moon comes steal - ing up be - hind the hill,_____

Breath-ing out up - on the air their sweet per - fume,__ Lives a dusk-y
Ev - 'ry-thing a - round me seems so calm and still,__ Save the gen-tle

94

Ida, Sweet as Apple Cider

Seems tho'___ can't live with-out you,___ Lis - ten,___ Oh! Hon-ey, do!___ I - da!___ I i-dol- ize yer,___ I love you, I - da, 'deed I do.___

Eleven Cent Cotton

A cry of anguish from the farmer, for whom a
low price for his cotton always spells misery.

Moderato

Words and Music by Bob Miller and Emma Dermer

1. 'Lev - en cent _ cot - ton, _ for - ty cent _ meat,
2. No corn in the crib, _ no chicks in the yard,

How _ in the world can a poor man _ eat? Pray _ for the sun - shine, _
No meat in the smoke house, no tubs full of lard; No cream in the pitch - er, no

'cause it will _ rain. _ Things _ get - tin' worse _ driv - in' all _ in - sane; _
hon - ey in the mug, No but - ter on the ta - ble and no 'las - ses in the jug; _

Eleven Cent Cotton

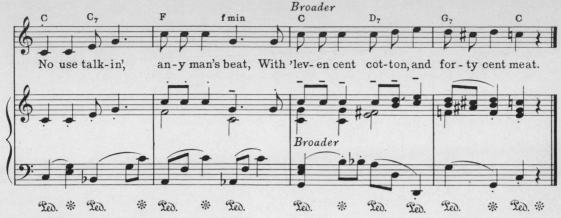

No use talk-in', an-y man's beat, With 'lev-en cent cot-ton, and for-ty cent meat.

3. 'Leven cent cotton, forty cent meat,
   How in the world can a poor man eat?
   Flour up high, cotton down low,
   How in the world can we raise the dough?
   Our clothes worn out, shoes run down,
   Old slouch hat with a hole in the crown.
   Back nearly broken, fingers all wore out,
   Cotton goin' down to rise no more.
   'Leven cent cotton, forty cent meat,
   Feels like a chain is on our feet.
   Poor getting poorer all around here,
   Kids coming regular ev'ry year;
   Planted corn, was a wheat year;
   Planted wheat and it turned a corn year.
   No use talkin', any man's beat,
   With 'leven cent cotton and forty cent meat.

4. 'Leven cent cotton, ten dollar pants,
   Who in the devil has got a chance?
   We can't buy clothes, we can't buy meat;
   Got too much cotton, not enough to eat.
   Can't help each other, what shall we do?
   I can't solve the problem so it's up to you;
   'Leven cent cotton, forty cent hose,
   Guess we will have to do without our clothes.
   'Leven cent cotton, forty cent meat,
   How in the world can a poor man eat?
   Mule's in the barn, the crop's laid by.
   The cup's plumb empty and the cow's gone dry;
   Well water's low, nearly out of sight,
   Can't take a bath on a Saturday night.
   No use talkin', any man's beat,
   With 'leven cent cotton and forty cent meat.

I Wonder Who's Kissing Her Now?

A song with the intimate, personal touch, characteristic of the early 1900's, and the hit song of Joe Howard at the Diamond Horseshoe, Billy Rose's famous New York night club.

Words by Will M. Hough and Frank R. Adams

Music by Joseph E. Howard

1. You have loved lots of girls in the sweet long a - go, And each
2. If you want to feel wretch-ed and lone - ly and blue, Just im -

one has meant Heav-en to you,_____ You have vow'd your af - fec - tion to
ag - ine the girl you love best_____ In the arms of some fel - low who's

each one in turn And have sworn to them all you'd be true;_____ You have
steal-ing a kiss From the lips that you once fond - ly pressed;_____ But the

how, _____ Won-der who's look-ing in - to her eyes,

Breath - ing sighs, tell - ing lies; I won-der who's buy-ing the wine____ For lips that I used to call mine,____ Won-der if she ev-er tells him of me, I won-der who's kiss-ing her now.____

The Crawdad

A fishing song, drowsy with the heat of the Texas sun. A crawdad is a crawfish used for bait and good for eating.

With an easy swing

1. Ah got a hook and you got a line, Hon - ey, _____
2. See'd a__ fel - ler tot - in' a sack, Hon - ey, _____

Ah got a hook and you got a line,
See'd a__ fel - ler tot - in' a sack,

Babe, _____ Ah got a hook and you got a line,
Babe, _____ See'd a__ fel - ler tot - in' a sack,

From Coleman-Bregman: *Songs of American Folks*, published by The John Day Co., New York.

Gwine-a ketch craw-dad sho' dis time, Hon-ey Babe.
Had all de craw-dad he could pack, Hon-ey Babe.

3. Sell mah crawdad three fo' a dime, Honey,
   Sell mah crawdad three fo' a dime, Babe,
   Sell mah crawdad three fo' a dime—
   Kin yo' sell yo's as cheap as mine, Honey Babe?

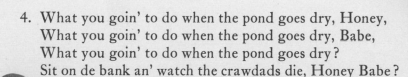

4. What you goin' to do when the pond goes dry, Honey,
   What you goin' to do when the pond goes dry, Babe,
   What you goin' to do when the pond goes dry?
   Sit on de bank an' watch the crawdads die, Honey Babe?

5. Dis is de end of mah crawdad song, Honey,
   Dis is de end of mah crawdad song, Babe,
   Dis is de end of mah crawdad song—
   Come on, Honey, better git along, Honey Babe.

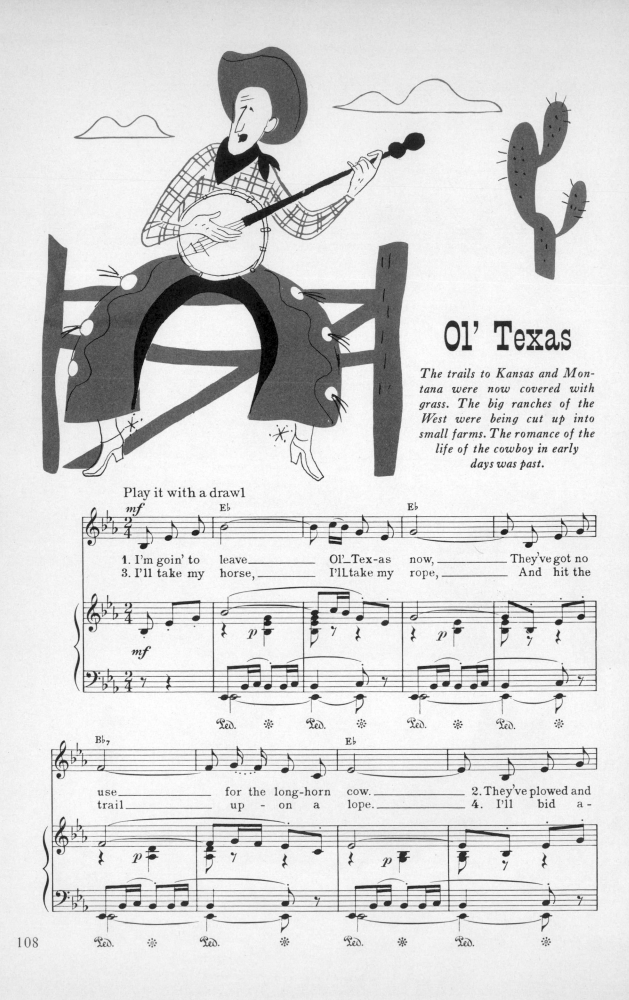

Ol' Texas

The trails to Kansas and Montana were now covered with grass. The big ranches of the West were being cut up into small farms. The romance of the life of the cowboy in early days was past.

Play it with a drawl

1. I'm goin' to leave_____ Ol' Tex-as now,_____ They've got no
3. I'll take my horse,_____ I'll take my rope,_____ And hit the

use_____ for the long-horn cow._____ 2. They've plowed and
trail_____ up-on a lope._____ 4. I'll bid a-

fenced_____ my_ cat - tle range,_____ And the peo - ple
dios_____ to the A - la - mo,_____ And_ turn my

there_____ are_ all so strange._____
head_____ toward Mex - i - co.

La Cucaracha

(THE COCKROACH)

"Cucaracha" may mean a cockroach or a little dried-up old maid, according to F. S. Curtis, Jr., of the Texas Folk Lore Society. The word was also used as a nickname for the late Venustiano Carranza. To understand the satire of "La Cucaracha," one must have a knowledge of the careers of Pancho Villa and Zapata and an acquaintance with Mexican political and revolutionary history.

rach - a, Ya no quier-e cam-i - nar, Por - que no
rach - a, Does - n't want to trav - el on, Be - cause she

tien - e, Por-que le fal - ta, Ma - ri - hua - na que fu - mar.
has - n't, Oh, no, she has - n't, Ma - ri - hua - na for to smoke.

2. All the girls up at Las Vegas
   Are most awful tall and skinny,
   But they're worse for plaintive pleading
   Than the souls in Purgatory.
   Chorus

3. All the girls here in the city
   Don't know how to give you kisses,
   While the ones from Albuquerque
   Stretch their necks to avoid misses.
   Chorus

4. One thing makes me laugh most hearty—
   Pancho Villa with no shirt on.
   Now the Carranzistas beat it
   Because Villa's men are coming.
   Chorus

5. Fellow needs an automobile
   If he undertakes the journey
   To the place to which Zapata
   Ordered the famous convention.
   Chorus

Big Rock Candy Mountains

With every depression men take to the railroads. The early years of the twentieth century saw tramps on every freight train, some looking for work and some, lured by fanciful tales told in hobo songs — such as in this old favorite — eager to try the wandering life.

One eve-ning, as the sun went down, And the jun-gle fires were burn-ing, Down the tracks came a ho-bo, hum-ming, And he

113

Big Rock Candy Mountains

land that's fair and bright, Where the hand-outs grow on
nev - er change your socks, And the lit - tle streams of

bush-es___ And you sleep out ev - 'ry night, Where the
al - ky-hol Come trick-ling down the rocks! The___

box-cars are all emp - ty And the sun shines ev - 'ry
shacks all have to tip their hats And the rail - road bulls are

114

day,   Oh,   the   birds and the bees and the
blind,   There's a   lake of ____ stew, and of

cig - a - rette   trees, ____   The rock - rye ___ springs where the
whis - key,   too, And you can pad - dle all a - round in a

whang doo - dle sings In the Big Rock Can - dy Moun - tains.''
big   can - oe In the Big Rock Can - dy Moun - tains.''

Kevin Barry

A song of the Irish Revolution of 1916. Irish boys and girls who first sang it here learned the ballad before they came to this country.

Gently but firmly

1. Ear- ly on a Mon-day morn - ing, High up on the gal-lows
2. Just be - fore he faced the hang-man In his lone - ly pris-on

tree, Kev- in Bar - ry gave his young life For the
cell, The Black and Tans tor- tured Bar - ry, Just be -

cause of lib-er-ty. On-ly a lad of eight-een
cause he would-n't tell The names of his brave

sum-mers, Still there's no one can de-ny, As he
com-rades, And oth-er things they wished to know. "Turn in-

walked to death that morn-ing No-bly held his head up high.
form-er and we'll free you!" But Kev-in proud-ly an-swered "No!"

3. "Shoot me like an Irish soldier.
Do not hang me like a dog,
For I fought to free old Ireland
On that still September morn,
All around the little bakery
Where we fought them hand to hand.
Shoot me like a brave soldier,
For I fought for Ireland."

St. Louis Blues

W. C. Handy's blues were inspired by the sayings of his own people. The inspiration for this, his most famous song, was the lament of a woman, wandering the streets of St. Louis, sorrowing for a faithless husband: "My man got a heart like a stone cast into the sea, and it's gone so far I can't reach it."

Words and Music by W. C. Handy

119

213

122

Or— else he—wouldn't have— gone— so— far— from me.—
I'll— love ma— ba - by— till— the— day— ah— die.—

spoken
Dog- gone it!

3. You ought to see dat stovepipe brown of mine,
   Lak he owns de Dimon' Joseph line.
   He'd make a cross-eyed o' man go stone blind,
   Blacker than midnight, teeth lak flags of truce,
   Blackest man in de whole St. Louis.
   Blacker de berry, sweeter is the juice.
   About a crap game he knows a pow'ful lot,
   But when work-time comes he's on de dot.
   Gwine to ask him for a cold ten-spot.
   What it takes to git it, he's certainly got.

CHORUS

A black-headed gal make a freight train jump the track.
Said a black-headed gal make a freight train jump the track,
But a long tall gal makes a preacher ball the jack.

EXTRA CHORUSES

Lawd, a blonde-headed woman makes a good man leave the town,
I said blonde-headed woman makes a good man leave the town,
But a red-head woman makes a boy slap his papa down.

O ashes to ashes and dust to dust,
I said ashes to ashes and dust to dust,
If my blues don't get you my jazzing must.

Conflict and Expansion

FROM 1850

THE years from the Civil War to the 1880's brought forth an odd mixture of songs. And it is only when we understand the complexities of the period itself that we realize how this mixture gives us an authentic picture of the times.

In the '50s, a bloody and terrible Civil War lay ahead. It would be fought over many well-recognized issues behind which were various less obvious economic factors. But in the eyes of the general public, *the* issue was slavery, pro or con, and the most typical songs of that day were those which focused attention on the Negro.

In the South, there were the Negro's own songs, the spirituals. Before the Civil War these were widely known, and perhaps were a prophecy of emancipation, since their theme was always freedom—thinly disguised as the "promised land," the "land of Canaan," or even the heaven where "everybody's goin'."

In the North, *Uncle Tom's Cabin* with its picture of Negro slavery whipped up popular sentiment as no book has ever done before or probably since. And throughout that part of the country, people were singing "My Darling Nelly Gray"—a sentimental account of a slave sold away from her home.

North and South, the popular and frivolous minstrel shows reflected this interest in the Negro. The comic songs presented a caricatured idea of the Negro, to be sure, and the sentimental songs were as "Uncle Tomish" as Uncle Tom himself. But their popularity showed an affection for the race and an awareness of it which had not existed before.

Stephen Foster, one of the foremost of our American song composers, revealed this growing feeling for the Negro in a letter to the famous minstrel E. P. Christy. One of Foster's most popular songs, "The Old Folks at Home," had been first published under Christy's name, with Foster's permission. Foster later claimed authorship, however, explaining to Christy that because of the strong prejudice against the "Ethiopian Song" he had been afraid that "Old Folks at Home" would injure his reputation. He had come to realize, however, that even the most refined people were developing a taste for Ethiopian songs. He attributed this largely to his own efforts to write suitable lyrics, rather than the "trashy, really offensive words which belong to songs of that order."

Foster was not, however, the only composer who popularized the minstrel song. James Bland, Christy himself, Dan Emmett (who gave us "Dixie"), and many others contributed to minstrel-song literature—and created one of our first, purely American forms of music.

When the Civil War came, song writers were concerned with one theme only. They uttered the bitterness and sense of guilt which involved the whole country. North and South, their songs were songs of self-justification, each side defending its own cause, each answering in paraphrase the songs of the other side. "Maryland, My Maryland," written by a Southerner imploring Maryland to secede, was promptly followed by a Northerner's appeal to "Belle Missouri, My Missouri," and this in turn by a Southern plea (since Missouri had not as yet taken sides) to "Missouri, Bright Land of the West." The famous "Bonnie Blue Flag," which celebrated secession, had its Northern parody:

"Hurrah! Hurrah! for equal rights, hurrah!
Hurrah for the brave old flag that bears the Stripes and Stars!"

Never had there been so many patriotic songs. Every great victory was celebrated. "Charleston Is Ours" was an ode to one triumph, "Richmond Is Ours" to another. The heroes had their place in music, too. The people sang to "Jefferson Davis" and of "General Beauregard's Grand March." They sang "Lincoln and Liberty" and "We're Coming, Father Abraham." It actually seemed as if the song writers were fighting the war among themselves.

Not all the songs, however, were so clearly earmarked for the North or the South, and some song writers were suspected of writing with a view to popularity on both sides. "Tenting Tonight" and "Just Before the Battle, Mother" were liked everywhere and applied equally well to either side. Then there was the curious situation where "Dixie," written by Dan Emmett, a Northerner, was taken as the South's own song, and "Battle Hymn of the Republic," based on "Say, Brothers, Will You Meet Us?"— a Southern camp-meeting tune—became the song of the Northern army.

As the guns ceased firing at the war's end, a great wave of jubilation seized the North. When the news of Lee's surrender reached the Eastern states at dawn, night-gowned men and women rushed out of their houses to embrace each other. Candles were lit in the windows, and around bonfires, fed with everything from old bedsteads to umbrellas and straw hats, they danced, singing "Rally Round the Flag."

But even this first joy was not a mellow joy, and soon a merciless revenge was to be visited upon the South. The Reconstruction Period which followed was to give rise to a new type of get-rich-quick exploiter in the South, and to a new and ruthless era for the whole country.

It was the day of political graft, of industrial progress, of rapid rises to fortune.

It was an age of vulgarity. In the political campaign between Grant and Seymour, the songs were unequaled for their crudity.

It was an age of drinking, and the quick release of spirits. Tavern songs sprang up. They were gay, they were catchy, but they reflected habits of conviviality which offended many. And their antidote, the temperance song, was born.

It was an age of shady hero-worship. The hobo song was popular, and the bandits of the opening West were the new Robin Hoods of their day. Nobody inspired as many songs as Jesse James and his brothers. Admiration for them was typical of the era.

It was, most of all, an age of expansion. Our lumber industry had always been large, but with the invention of the steam-driven circular saw it grew in leaps and bounds. Something about the isolation, the masculinity, of the lumber camp inspired a special language of its own. A mythology, entirely American in flavor, grew up about lumbering, but the songs of the lumberjacks were American, Irish, Scottish, and French-Canadian, as were the men themselves.

Our railroads spanned the country, increasing from 30,000 miles of track to 200,000 in a short period. The Erie, the Pennsylvania, the Baltimore & Ohio, and the Illinois Central lines were completed. It was the Railroad Age, and we began to encourage immigration to import cheap labor for the work. Fifteen million immigrants responded to our inducements; hordes of Irish and Italians, Poles, Scots, Germans, and Swedes increased our laboring population, bringing with them their own songs to add to our culture.

In a growing West, the cowboy began to develop his own music. As cattle were rounded up in Texas and driven north to meet the approaching railroad, a whole song literature of the trail was born. The cowboy sang to beguile the long evenings around the campfire or to banish loneliness as he rode the trail. The tunes came from English and Scottish ballads and from popular American songs of the day. They were sentimental, but the cowboy gave the words reality as he sang of little dogies and roundups and the wide plains.

But neither the songs of a growing America nor the rowdy tavern music was wholly typical of the period. The great mass of people in the East were settled and respectable, even excessively so. Their respectability would not permit them to haunt the taverns or the music halls or the theatres. They sponsored Father Kempes' Ye Old Folkes' Concerts, which toured the states giving musical performances, in colonial costume, and they attended concerts given by family groups such as the Peaks, the Bergers, the Hutchinsons, who sang religious songs and a few of the more subdued ballads. But for any other entertainment, the young folk and the old folk, too, met at each other's homes. There they played charades, made fudge, and gathered around the piano to sing, learning the words of the latest popular music from penny broadsheets bought at the street corners.

Some of the songs they sang were gay, but the songs they loved best were the sentimental ones, the excessively genteel "tear jerkers," such ditties as "White Wings" and "Silver Threads Among the Gold." Perhaps the period of easy money also inspired easy tears, or perhaps as one writer has suggested the men having gone West to seek new opportunities, the East was dominated by women who gloried in sentimental respectability.

Even the religious songs of the period were prey to sentimentality. The revival meetings of the time were genuine enough, but the Moody and Sankey songs were vulgar and saccharine. And Sankey was not the only offender. "Moody and Sankey" became a generic term for a certain type of gospel song which other composers contributed to the tearful emotionalism of the revival meetings.

In fact, that saccharinity is what we are most apt to remember when we think of the '80's, forgetting the virile work songs and the gayer music of tavern and music hall. But perhaps sentimentality was only one phase of the raw spirit in the American people, which elsewhere was being translated into the sturdy, powerful growth of a still young United States.

Pick a Bale of Cotton

A work song of the cotton pickers. Lead Belly said of it: "If anything could help a man pick a bale of cotton (fifteen hundred heavy pounds!) in a day, it would be this merry, swaggering song." The same tremendous lie is repeated in every stanza, he said, but it is a good lie and hurts nobody, since every cotton picker knows it never was the truth and never could be.

Words and Melody adapted and arranged by John A. and Alan Lomax

1. You got to jump down, turn a-round, Pick uh bale uh cot-ton, Got to
2. Me an' my part-ner can Pick uh bale uh cot-ton, Oh—

jump down, turn a-round, To pick uh bale uh day.
me an' my part-ner can— Pick uh bale uh day.

O, Lawd-y,

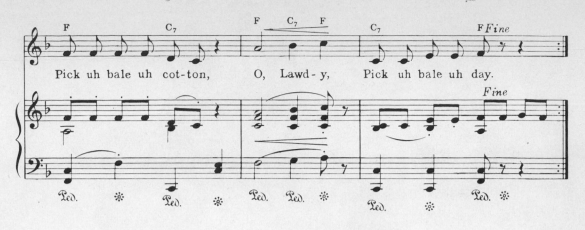

Pick uh bale uh cot-ton, O, Lawd-y, Pick uh bale uh day.

3. Me an' my wife can
   Pick uh bale uh cotton,
   Oh, me an' my wife can
   Pick uh bale uh day.
   Chorus

4. Had uh little woman could
   Pick uh bale uh cotton,
   Oh, had uh little woman could
   Pick uh bale uh day.
   Chorus

5. I b'lieve to my soul I can
   Pick uh bale uh cotton,
   I b'lieve to my soul I can
   Pick uh bale uh day.
   Chorus

6. Went to Corsicana to
   Pick uh bale uh cotton,
   Oh, went to Corsicana to
   Pick uh bale uh day.
   Chorus

CHORUS

O, lawdy,
Pick uh bale uh cotton,
O, lawdy,
Pick uh bale uh day.

Jacob's Ladder

An early Negro spiritual.

Exultantly

1. We are climb-ing Ja-cob's lad-der, We are
2. Ev-'ry round goes high-er, high-er, Ev-'ry

3. Sinner, do you love my Jesus? *(3 times)*
   Soldiers of the cross.

4. If you love Him, why not serve Him? *(3 times)*
   Soldiers of the cross.

5. We are climbing higher, higher, *(3 times)*
   Soldiers of the cross.

Darling Nelly Gray

Slaves were sold by their masters and transported from plantation to plantation, from state to state. Families were frequently separated. This song about a slave sold away from her home was tremendously popular in the North during the Civil War.

Words and Music by B. R. Hanby

1. There's a low green valley on the old Ken-tuck-y shore, There I've whiled man-y hap-py hours a-way. A sit-ting and a-sing-ing by the

2. One night I went to see her but "she's gone," the neigh-bors say, The white man bound her with his chain, They have tak-en her to Geor-gia for to

lit - tle cot-tage door, Where_ lived my_ dar-ling Nel-ly Gray.
wear her life a - way, As she toils in the cot-ton and the cane.

Chorus

Oh! my poor Nel-ly Gray, they have tak-en you a - way, And I'll

nev-er see my dar-ling an-y more. I'm a - sit-ting by the riv-er and I'm

weep-ing all the day, For you've gone from the old Ken-tuck-y shore.

My Old Kentucky Home

Before "Old Folks at Home" was published (1851), Stephen Foster had never been south of the Ohio River. "My Old Kentucky Home" romanticizes the life of the Southern Negro.

Words and Music by Stephen Foster

1. The sun shines bright on the old Ken-tuck-y home, 'Tis
— young folks roll on the lit-tle cab-in floor, All

sum-mer, the dark-ies are gay; The corn - top's ripe and the
mer-ry, all hap-py, and bright; By'n'- by hard times comes a -

mead-ow's in the bloom, While the birds make mu - sic all the day; The
knock-ing at the door, Then, my old Ken-tuck-y home, good-night!

Chorus

Weep no more, my la - dy, Oh!

My Old Kentucky Home

weep no more to-day! We will sing one song for the

old Ken-tuck-y home, For the old Ken-tuck-y home, far a-way.

slower

2. They hunt no more for the 'possum and the 'coon
   On the meadow, the hill, and the shore;
   They sing no more by the glimmer of the moon,
   On the bench by the old cabin door;
   The day goes by like a shadow o'er the heart,
   With sorrow where all was delight;
   The time has come when the darkies have to part,
   Then, my old Kentucky home, good-night!
   Chorus

3. The head must bow and the back will have to bend,
   Wherever the darky may go;
   A few more days and the trouble all will end,
   In the fields where the sugar-canes grow;
   A few more days for to tote the weary load,
   No matter, 'twill never be light;
   A few more days till we totter on the road,
   Then, my old Kentucky home, good-night!
   Chorus

Nelly Bly

A rare type of Foster song—a whimsical Negro love song.

Allegro

Words and Music by Stephen Foster

1. Nel-ly Bly! Nel-ly Bly! bring de broom a-long, We'll
2. Nel-ly Bly hab a voice like a tur-tle dove, I

sweep de kit-chen clean, my dear, and hab a lit-tle song.
hear it in de mead-ow and I hear it in de grove.

Heigh! Nel - ly, Ho! Nel - ly, lis - ten, lub, to me, I'll

sing for you, play for you, a dul - cem mel - o - dy.

3. Nelly Bly shuts her eye when she goes to sleep.
   When she wakens up again her eyeballs 'gin to peep.
   De way she walks, she lifts her foot, and den she bump it down.
   And when it lights, dere's music dah in dat part ob de town.
   Chorus

4. Nelly Bly! Nelly Bly! Nebber, nebber sigh;
   Nebber bring de tear drop to de corner ob your eye.
   For de pie is made ob punkins and de mush is made ob corn,
   And dere's corn and punkins plenty, lub, a-lyin' in de barn.
   Chorus

CHORUS

Heigh! Nelly, Ho! Nelly, listen, lub, to me.
I'll sing for you, play for you, a dulcem melody.
Heigh! Nelly, Ho! Nelly, listen, lub, to me.
I'll sing for you, play for you, a dulcem melody.

Old Abe Lincoln

*A famous campaign song in the exciting Presidential election of 1860. The tune is
from the Negro spiritual "Ol' Gray Mare Come Tearin' Out de Wilderness."
"The Old Gray Mare, She Ain't What She Used to Be" is derived
from the same spiritual.*

Allegro moderato

1. Old Abe Lin-coln came out of the wil-der-ness,
2. Old Jeff Da-vis tore down the gov-ern-ment,

Out of the wil-der-ness, out of the wil-der-ness, Old Abe Lin-coln came
Tore down the gov-ern-ment, tore down the gov-ern-ment, Old Jeff Da-vis

out of the wil-der-ness, Down in Il-li-nois.
tore down the gov-ern-ment, Man-y long years a-go.

3. But old Abe Lincoln built up a better one,
   Built up a better one, built up a better one;
   Old Abe Lincoln built up a better one,
   Many long years ago.

140

The Bonnie Blue Flag

This was the national anthem of the Confederates during the Civil War. The "Bonnie Blue Flag," a blue flag with a single white star in the center, was adopted by South Carolina, the first of the Southern states to secede. Richard Barksdale Harwell says it is reported that General Ben F. Butler confiscated the music plates, fined A. E. Blackmar, its publisher, and threatened to punish any Rebel heard whistling or singing the song.

1. We are a band of broth-ers, and na-tive to the soil,___ Fight-ing for our Lib-er-ty with treas-ure, blood, and toil;___ And
2. As long as the old Un-ion was faith-ful to her trust,___ Like friends___ and like broth-ers,___ kind were we and just;___ But

when our rights were threat-'ned, the cry rose near and far:___ Hur-
now, when North-ern treach-'ry at - tempts our rights to mar,___ We

rah! for the Bon-nie Blue Flag, that bears a Sin - gle Star.___
hoist___ the Bon-nie Blue Flag, that bears a Sin - gle Star.___

f Chorus

Hur - rah!___ Hur - rah!___ for South-ern Rights, Hur - rah!___ Hur-

rah! for the Bon-nie Blue Flag, that bears a Sin - gle Star.

Battle Hymn of the Republic

The tune of the "Battle Hymn" dates back at least to 1856, and is credited to a Southern com-
poser, William Steffe. It was first sung to the words "Say, brothers, will you meet us?" and
this Southern camp-meeting song was a favorite with American soldiers before the Civil
War. After the Harpers Ferry incident in 1859, the words "John Brown's body lies a-
moldering in the grave" were substituted; and when the Confederacy was formed, a parody,
"We will hang Jeff Davis to a sour apple tree," was sung to the same tune. In 1861 Julia
Ward Howe, visiting some army camps outside Washington, heard the soldiers march into
battle stirringly singing "John Brown's Body." That night she wrote for the old camp-meeting
tune the words of the "Battle Hymn," which became the great marching song of the North.

Maestoso

Words by Julia Ward Howe

Battle Hymn of the Republic

Tramp! Tramp! Tramp!

George F. Root, an important composer of the Civil War period, made his greatest contribution, perhaps, in the writing of war songs. His "Tramp, Tramp, Tramp," a famous marching song of the Northern armies, is still considered one of our best military tunes.

Words and Music by G. F. Root

Allegro moderato

1. In the pris - on cell I sit, Think - ing,
2. In the bat - tle front we stood, When their

Tramp! Tramp! Tramp!

moth- er dear, of you, And our bright and hap- py home so far a-
fierc- est charge they made, And they swept us off a hun- dred men or

way; And the tears they fill my eyes, Spite of
more; But be - fore we reached their lines They were

all that I can do, Though I try to cheer my com-rades and be gay.
beat-en back, dis-mayed, And we heard the cry of vic- t'ry o'er and o'er.

Chorus

Tramp, tramp, tramp! the boys are march - - ing,

Cheer up, com-rades, they will come, And be-neath the star-ry flag we shall breathe the air a-gain Of the free land in our own be-lov-ed home.

3. So within the prison cell,
   We are waiting for the day
   That shall come to open wide the iron door;
   And the hollow eye grows bright,
   And the poor heart almost gay,
   As we think of seeing home and friends once more.

CHORUS

Tramp, tramp, tramp! the boys are marching,
Cheer up, comrades, they will come (they will come)
And beneath the starry flag we shall breathe the air again
Of the free land in our own beloved home.

Tenting Tonight

Walter Kittredge's "Tenting Tonight" was sung by civilians and soldiers, North and South. The general war weariness is reflected here, as it was in so many of the Civil War songs.

Words and Music by Walter Kittredge

1. We're tent-ing to-night on the old camp ground,
2. We've been tent-ing to-night on the old camp ground,

Give us a song to cheer Our wea-ry hearts, a
Think-ing of days gone by, Of the loved ones at home that

song of home And friends we loved so dear.
gave us the hand, And the tear that said, "Good-bye!"

Chorus

Man-y are the hearts that are wea-ry to-night, Wish-ing for the war to cease;

Man-y are the hearts that are look-ing for the right, To see the dawn of peace.

Tent-ing to-night, tent-ing to-night, Tent-ing on the old camp ground.

3. We are tired of war on the old camp ground,
Many are dead and gone
Of the brave and true who've left their home,
Others been wounded long ago.
Chorus

4. We've been fighting tonight on the old camp ground,
Many are lying near;
Some are dead, and some are dying,
Many are in tears.
Chorus

152

Just Before the Battle, Mother

*An early, sentimental war song which, like "Tenting Tonight,"
was sung by Civil War soldiers of both sides.*

Words and Music by G. F. Root

153

Chorus

Fare - - well, Moth - er, you may nev - er
Press me to your heart a - gain; But oh, you'll not for - get me,
Moth - er, _____ If I'm num - bered with the slain.

Listen to the Mocking Bird

Words and Music by Alice Hawthorne

Listen to the Mocking Bird

Septimus Winner's famous poem was published in 1855 under the pseudonym "Alice Hawthorne." The cheerful, whistling tune he is said to have credited to a little Negro boy, Richard Milburn, whom he heard whistling it. The song was tremendously popular during the war period, and people danced to it on the White House lawn when the news of Lee's surrender was received. It was sung in family drawing rooms throughout the 19th century.

dies. She's sleep-ing in the val-ley, The
side. 'Twas in the mild Sep-tem-ber, Sep-

val-ley, the val-ley, She's sleep-ing in the
tem-ber, Sep-tem-ber, 'Twas in the mild Sep-

val-ley, And the mock-ing bird is sing-ing where she lies.
tem-ber, And the mock-ing bird is sing-ing far and wide.

157

Chorus
F F C7 C7 C7 F F
Lis-ten to the mock-ing bird, Lis-ten to the mock-ing bird, The
pp pp mf
C C7 F F
mock-ing bird is sing-ing o'er her grave; Lis-ten to the
F C7 C7 C7 F D
mock-ing bird, Lis-ten to the mock-ing bird, Still
pp pp mf
g min C7 F
sing-ing where the weep-ing wil-lows wave.
L. H. R. H.

Shoo Fly, Don't Bother Me

A nonsense song of the Civil War and a great favorite among the Negro troops.

Lively
Chorus

Shoo, fly, don't both-er me! Shoo, fly, don't both-er me!

Shoo, fly, don't both-er me, I be-long to Comp-'ny G.

Verse

I feel, I feel, I feel, I feel like a morn-ing star, I
I feel, I feel, I feel, That's what my— moth-er said, Like

feel, I feel, I feel, I feel like a morn-ing star.
an-gels pour-ing 'las-ses down, right down up-on my head.

Wake Nicodemus

During his childhood, Work probably heard many songs and stories of
plantation life from the runaway slaves hiding in his father's station
of the Underground Railroad. The romantic figure of Nicodemus may
easily have grown out of these tales.

Allegro moderato

Words and Music by Henry C. Work

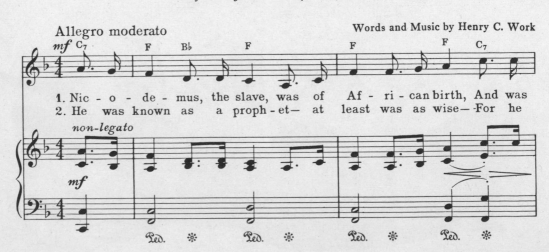

1. Nic - o - de - mus, the slave, was of Af - ri - can birth, And was
2. He was known as a proph-et— at least was as wise— For he

bought for a bag-ful of gold; He was reck-on'd as part of the
told of the bat-tles to come; And he trem-bled with dread when he

salt of the earth, But he died years a-go, ver-y old. 'Twas his
rolled up his eyes, And we heed-ed the shake of his thumb. Though he

last sad re-quest— so we laid him a-way In the
clothed us with fear, yet the gar-ments he wore Were in

Wake Nicodemus

trunk of an old hol-low tree. "Wake me up!" was his charge, "at the
patch-es at el-bow and knee; And he still wears the suit, that he

first break of day— Wake me up for the great Ju-bi-lee!"
used to of yore, And he sleeps in the old hol-low tree!

Chorus

The "Good Time Com-ing" is al-most here! It was long, long, long on the

way! Now run and tell E-li-jah to hur-ry up Pomp, And

meet us at the gum-tree down in the swamp, To wake Nic - o - de - mus to-day.

3. Nicodemus was never the sport of the lash,
Though the bullet has oft cross'd his path;
There were none of his masters so brave or so rash,
As to face such a man in his wrath.
Yet his great heart with kindness was filled to the brim—
He obeyed who was born to command;
But he long'd for the morning which then was so dim—
For the morning which now is at hand.
Chorus

4. 'Twas a long weary night—we were almost in fear
That the future was more than he knew;
'Twas a long weary night—but the morning is near,
And the words of our prophet are true.
There are signs in the sky that the darkness is gone—
There are tokens in endless array;
While the storm which had seemingly banished the dawn,
Only hastens the advent of day.
Chorus

CHORUS

The "Good Time Coming" is almost here!
It was long, long, long on the way!
Now run and tell Elijah to hurry up Pomp,
And meet us at the gum-tree down in the swamp,
To wake Nicodemus today.

163

Little Brown Church in the Vale

In Bradford, Iowa, during Civil War days, the pioneers built a church. It was begun in 1859 and completed and dedicated in 1864, just before Christmas. The materials and labor were contributed by the pioneers. Dr. Pitts, who lived not far from Bradford, helped in the construction of the church. The church and the song he wrote about it have become famous. More than 40,000 people visit the church yearly.

Words and Music by William S. Pitts

1. There's a church in the val-ley by the wild-wood, No love-li-er place in the dale; No spot is so dear to my child-hood As the lit-tle brown church in the vale.

2. How sweet on a bright Sab-bath morn-ing, To list to the clear ring-ing bell; Its tones so sweet are call-ing Oh, come to the church in the vale.

Chorus

Oh, come to the church in the wild-wood, Oh, come to the church in the dale, No spot is so dear to my child-hood As the lit-tle brown church in the vale.

Oh, Freedom

After the war, Negroes sang openly of freedom, not only of freedom in the world to come, as they had done in slavery days, but of a personal freedom here and now.

Slowly, but with jubilation

1. Oh, free-dom! Oh, free-dom!
2. No more moan-in', No more moan-in',

Oh, free-dom o-ver me!
No more moan-in' o-ver me!
An' be-fore I'd be a slave, I'll be
bur-ied in my grave, An' go home to my Lord an' be free.

3. There'll be singin', there'll be singin',
There'll be singin' over me.
An' before I'd be a slave
I'll be buried in my grave,
An' go home to my Lord an' be free.

4. There'll be shoutin', there'll be shoutin',
There'll be shoutin' over me.
An' before I'd be a slave
I'll be buried in my grave,
An' go home to my Lord an' be free.

167

We Three Kings

The Pilgrim Fathers, adhering to the Puritan view, discouraged
Christmas celebrations of any kind. Carol singing, therefore, was a
fairly late activity in America. "We Three Kings," one of our most
beautiful carols, was written about 1857.

Words and Music by John H. Hopkins

Note: Stanzas 2, 3, and 4 are sung by Melchior, Caspar, and Balthazar respectively.

Star of night, Star with roy-al beau-ty bright, West-ward
lead-ing, still pro-ceed-ing, Guide us to Thy per-fect light.

CASPAR:

3. Frankincense to offer have I,
   Incense owns a Deity nigh,
   Prayer and praising, all men raising,
   Worship Him, God most high.
   Chorus

BALTHAZAR:

4. Myrrh is mine, its bitter perfume
   Breathes a life of gathering gloom,
   Sorrowing, sighing, bleeding, dying,
   Sealed in the stone cold tomb.
   Chorus

5. Glorious now, behold Him arise,
   King and God and sacrifice,
   Alleluia, Alleluia,
   Earth to the heavens replies.

CHORUS

O Star of wonder, Star of night,
Star with royal beauty bright,
Westward leading, still proceeding,
Guide us to Thy perfect light.

Where Is My Boy Tonight?

Rev. Robert Lowry, pastor of the Hanson Place Baptist Church, Brooklyn, did much to promote the gospel-song movement. He wrote a number of songs, the best known of which are "Shall We Gather by the River?" and "Where Is My Boy Tonight?"

Words and Music by Robert Lowry

With feeling

1. Where is my wan - d'ring boy to - night, The
2. Once he was pure as morn - ing dew, As he

boy of my ten - d'rest care, The boy that was once my
knelt at his moth - er's knee; No face was so bright, no

Where Is My Boy Tonight?

172

Nearer, My God, to Thee

"Nearer, My God, to Thee" was written by Lowell Mason in 1856. Mason, well-known writer of many beautiful hymns, devoted himself during the latter part of his life to the introduction of music into the public schools. It was he who gained the right for every child to receive elementary music instruction at public expense.

Words by Sarah F. Adams

Music by Lowell Mason

1. Near-er, my God, to Thee, Near-er to Thee! E'en though it
2. Though like the wan-der-er, The sun gone down, Dark-ness be

174

be   a cross   That—rais-eth   me;   Still   all   my   song   shall be,
o - ver me,   My—rest a   stone,   Yet   in   my   dreams   I'd   be

Near - er,   my   God,   to   Thee,   Near - er,   my   God,   to Thee,   Near - er   to   Thee!
Near - er,   my   God,   to   Thee,   Near - er,   my   God,   to Thee,   Near - er   to   Thee!

3. There let the way appear,
   Steps unto heaven;
   All that Thou sendest me
   In mercy given;
   Angels to beckon me
   Nearer, my God, to Thee, etc.

4. Then with my waking thoughts
   Bright with Thy praise,
   Out of my stony griefs
   Bethel I'll raise;
   So by my woes to be
   Nearer, my God, to Thee, etc.

5. Or if on joyful wing,
   Cleaving the sky,
   Sun, moon, and stars forgot,
   Upwards I fly,
   Still all my song shall be
   Nearer, my God, to Thee, etc.

In the Sweet By and By

A gospel hymn. After the Civil War, people again felt the need, as they had in the early colonial days, for religious songs "more to the popular liking" than the strict hymnody of the churches, and gospel hymns became increasingly popular.

Words by S. Fillmore Bennett

Music by J. P. Webster

1. There's a land that is fair - er than day, And by faith we can see it a - far, For the Fa - ther waits o - ver the way, To pre - pare us a dwell - ing place there.

2. We shall sing on that beau - ti - ful shore The mel - o - di - ous songs of the blest, And our spir - its shall sor - row no more, Not a sigh for the bless - ing of rest.

Chorus

In the sweet by and by We shall
meet on that beau-ti-ful shore; In the sweet by and
by We shall meet on that beau-ti-ful shore.

3. To our bountiful Father above
   We will offer the tribute of praise
   For the glorious gift of His love,
   And the blessings that hallow our days.

CHORUS

In the sweet by and by
We shall meet on that beautiful shore;
In the sweet by and by
We shall meet on that beautiful shore.

177

The Old Oaken Bucket

The words of this much-loved song were written as early as 1818 and were first sung to a Scottish air, "Jessie, the Flower o' Dumblane." The tune which is so familiar today was written by an English composer, George Kiallmark, and first published in 1870.

Words by Samuel Woodworth

Music by George Kiallmark

1. How dear to my heart are the scenes of my child-hood, When fond rec-ol-lec-tion pre-sents them to view!
   The or-chard, the mead-ow, the deep tan-gled wild-wood, And ev-'ry loved spot which my in-fan-cy knew;
   The wide-spread-ing pond and the mill that stood

by it, The bridge and the rock where the cat-a-ract fell;

The cot of my fa-ther, the dair-y house
The old oak-en buck-et, the i-ron bound

nigh it, And e'en the rude buck-et that hung in the well.
buck-et, The moss-cov-ered buck-et that hung in the well.

2. The moss-covered bucket I hailed as a treasure,
   For often at noon when returned from the field,
   I found it the source of an exquisite pleasure,
   The purest and sweetest that nature can yield.
   How ardent I seized it with hands that were glowing,
   And quick to the white-pebbled bottom it fell;
   Then soon, with the emblem of truth overflowing
   And dripping with coolness, it rose from the well.
   The old oaken bucket, the iron-bound bucket,
   The moss-covered bucket that hung in the well.

The Quilting Party

*Quilting parties provided an excellent opportunity for young and old
to meet. Quilts were a necessity and social gatherings important. Perhaps
the best part of the evening was "seeing Nellie home."*

home.
home.

I was see-ing Nel-lie home, — I was see-ing Nel-lie

home; And 'twas from Aunt Di-nah's quilt-ing par-ty, I was see-ing Nel-lie home.

3. On my lips a whisper trembled,
Trembled 'till it dared to come.
And 'twas from Aunt Dinah's quilting party,
I was seeing Nellie home.
Chorus

4. On my life new hopes were dawning,
And those hopes have lived and grown.
And 'twas from Aunt Dinah's quilting party,
I was seeing Nellie home.
Chorus

CHORUS
I was seeing Nellie home.
I was seeing Nellie home;
And 'twas from Aunt Dinah's quilting party,
I was seeing Nellie home.

When You and I Were Young, Maggie

This song is a true story of Maggie Clark, who lived in Canada and was courted by her school-teacher, George W. Johnson. They were married in 1865, but their dream of a long romance did not come true, for Maggie died that same year.

Words by George W. Johnson

Music by J. A. Butterfield

1. I wan-der'd to-day to the hill, Mag-gie, To watch the scene be-low; The creek and the creak-ing old mill, Mag-gie, As we used to long a-go. The

2. A cit-y so si-lent and lone, Mag-gie, Where the young and the gay and the best, In pol-ished white man-sions of stone, Mag-gie, Have each found a place of rest, Is

When You and I Were Young, Maggie

green grove is gone from the hill, Mag-gie, Where
built where the birds used to play, Mag-gie, And

first the dai-sies sprung; The creak-ing old mill is
join in the songs that were sung; For we sang as gay as

still, Mag-gie, since you and I were young.
they, Mag-gie, When you and I were young.

Chorus

And now we are a-ged and gray, Mag-gie, And the

When You and I Were Young, Maggie

tri - als of life___ near-ly done; Let us sing of the days that are

gone, Mag-gie, When you and___ I were___ young.

3. They say I am feeble with age, Maggie,
   My steps are less sprightly than then;
   My face is a well-written page, Maggie,
   But time alone was the pen.
   They say we are aged and gray, Maggie,
   As spray by the white breakers flung;
   But to me you're fair as you were, Maggie,
   When you and I were young.

CHORUS

And now we are aged and gray, Maggie,
And the trials of life nearly done;
Let us sing of the days that are gone, Maggie,
When you and I were young.

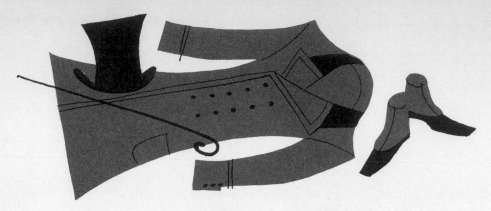

Soldier, Soldier, Won't You Marry Me?

*A Kentucky version of an English folk song widely sung after
the demobilization of the soldiers of the Civil War.*

1. Now, now, sol-dier, won't you mar-ry me? For O the fife and drum. How can I mar-ry such a pret-ty girl as you when I've got no hat to put on?

2. Off to the hat-shop she did go As hard as she could run; Got him a hat and all fine things, Now sol-dier put them on.

Last Verse

7. Now, now, sol - dier, won't you mar - ry___ me? For O the fife and drum._____ How can I mar - ry such a pret - ty girl as you, And a wife and a ba - by at home?

3. "Now, now, soldier, won't you marry me?
    For O the fife and drum."
    "How can I marry such a pretty girl as you
    When I've got no coat to put on?"

4. Off to the tailor she did go
    As hard as she could run;
    Got him a coat and all fine things.
    Now, soldier, put them on.

5. "Now, now, soldier, won't you marry me?
    For O the fife and drum."
    "How can I marry such a pretty girl as you
    When I've got no shoes to put on?"

6. Off to the shoe-shop she did go
    As hard as she could run;
    Got him shoes and all fine things.
    Now, soldier, put them on.

7. "Now, now, soldier, won't you marry me?
    For O the fife and drum."
    "How can I marry such a pretty girl as you,
    And a wife and baby at home?"

187

March of the Men of Harlech

*In 1486 the Earl of Pembroke was sent by Edward IV to storm
Harlech Castle, a Welsh stronghold. This march, written years later
to commemorate that battle, is known almost as
well in America as in Wales.*

1. { Men of Har-lech! In the Hol-low, Do ye hear like rush-ing bil - low,
'Tis the tramp of Sax-on foe-men, Sax-on spear-men, Sax-on bow-men,

Wave on wave that surg-ing fol - low Bat-tle's dis-tant sound?
Be they knights, or hinds, or yeo-men, They shall bite the ground!

Loose the folds a - sun-der,   Flag we con-quer un-der!   The

pla - cid sky now bright on high Shall launch its bolts in thun-der!

On-ward! 'tis the coun-try needs us. He is brav-est, he who leads us!

Broader *a tempo*

Hon - or's self now proud-ly heads us, Free-dom! God and Right!

2. Rocky steeps and passes narrow
    Flash with spear and flight of arrow.
    Who would think of death or sorrow?
    Death is glory now!
    Hurl the reeling horsemen over,
    Let the earth dead foemen cover!
    Fate of friend, of wife, of lover,
    Trembles on a blow!

    Strands of life are riven!
    Blow for blow is given
    In deadly lock, or battle shock,
    And mercy shrieks to heaven!
    Men of Harlech! young or hoary,
    Would you win a name in story?
    Strike for home, for life, for glory!
    Freedom! God and Right!

189

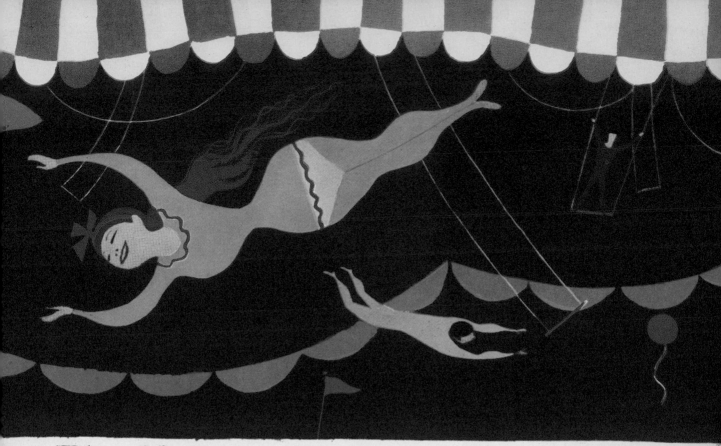

The Man on the Flying Trapeze

*A circus song of 1868. Variety-hall and tavern entertainments of the
time were considered too rough for women and children, but the circus
was a pleasant amusement which could be enjoyed by everyone.*

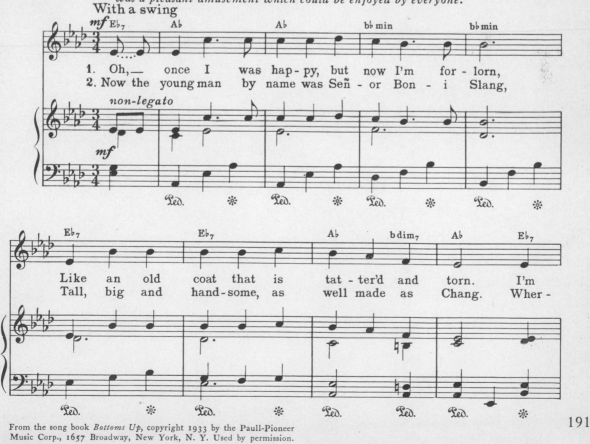

1. Oh,— once I was hap-py, but now I'm for-lorn,
2. Now the young man by name was Señ - or Bon - i Slang,

Like an old coat that is tat - ter'd and torn. I'm
Tall, big and hand-some, as well made as Chang. Wher -

From the song book *Bottoms Up*, copyright 1933 by the Paull-Pioneer
Music Corp., 1657 Broadway, New York, N. Y. Used by permission.

left in this wide world to fret and to mourn, Be -
e'er he ap - peared, how the hall loud - ly rang, With o -

trayed by a maid in her teens._____ Now this girl that I
va - tions from all peo - ple there._____ He'd_ smile from the

loved, she was hand-some and swell, And I tried all I knew her to
bar on the peo - ple be - low And_ one night he smiled on my

please; _____ But I nev - er could please her one quar - ter so
love, _____ She winked back at him, and she shout - ed "Bra -

well, As that man on the fly - ing tra - peze. _____
vo!" As he hung by his nose from a - bove. _____

poco rit.

Chorus
a tempo

He flies thro' the air with the great - est of ease, The

a tempo

193

The Man on the Flying Trapeze

dar - ing young man on the fly - ing tra - peze. His

move-ments are grace-ful; all girls he does please, And my

love he's pur - loin - éd a - way. _____

3. Her father and mother were both on my side
   And tried very hard to make her my bride.
   Her father, he sighed, and her mother, she cried
   To see her throw herself away.
   'Twas all no avail, she went there ev'ry night
   And threw her bouquets on the stage,
   Which caused him to meet her—how he ran me down,
   To tell it would take a whole page.
   Chorus

4. One night I as usual went to her dear home,
   And found there her mother and father alone.
   I asked for my love, and soon 'twas made known,
   To my horror, that she'd run away.
   She packed up her boxes and eloped in the night,
   With him with the greatest of ease.
   From two stories high he had lowered her down
   To the ground on his flying trapeze.
   Chorus

5. Some months after that I went into a hall;
   To my surprise I found there on the wall
   A bill in red letters which did my heart gall,
   That she was appearing with him.
   He'd taught her gymnastics, and dressed her in tights
   To help him live at his ease.
   He'd made her assume a masculine name,
   And now she goes on the trapeze.

FINAL CHORUS

She floats through the air with the greatest of ease;
You'd think her a man on the flying trapeze.
She does all the work while he takes his ease,
And that's what's become of my love.

O Tannenbaum

Sigmund Spaeth says that this may be one of the oldest tunes in existence today, and may have been the tune used for the drinking song "Mihi est Propositum," written in the 12th century. By 1824 it was sung in Germany to the words of a Christmas carol, "Tannenbaum, O Tannenbaum," and it was in this form that it became known and loved in America. During the Civil War the tune was used for one of the most famous of the Confederate songs, "Maryland, My Maryland."

English version by Freda Morrill Abrams

O Tan-nen-baum, O Tan-nen-baum! wie treu sind dei - ne
O Ev - er-green, O Ev - er - green! How faith-ful are your

Blät - ter! Du grünst nicht nur zur Som - mer - zeit; nein,
branch - es! They're green when sum - mer days are bright; They're

auch im Win - ter wenn es schneit. O Tan - nen-baum, O
green when win - ter snow is white. O Ev - er-green, O

Tan - nen-baum! wie treu sind dei - ne Blät - ter!
Ev - er-green! How faith - ful are your branch - es!

2. O Evergreen, O Evergreen!
   You give us so much pleasure!
   How oft at Christmas-tide the sight,
   O green fir tree, gives us delight!
   O Evergreen, O Evergreen!
   You give us so much pleasure!

3. O Evergreen, O Evergreen!
   Your loyal dress does teach me,
   Does teach of hope and constancy,
   As seasons pass you strengthen me.
   O Evergreen, O Evergreen!
   Your loyal dress does teach me!

Little Brown Jug

One of the best known of all drinking songs. It is believed to have been written—both words and music—by Joseph E. Winner.

1. My wife and I lived all a-lone, In a lit-tle log hut we call'd our own;
2. 'Tis you who makes my friends and foes, 'Tis you who makes me wear old clothes;

She loved gin and I loved rum, I tell you we had lots of fun.
Here you are so near my nose, so tip her up and down she goes.

Chorus

Ha! ha! ha! you and me, Lit-tle brown jug don't I love thee!

Ha! ha! ha! you and me, Lit-tle brown jug don't I love thee!

3. When I go toiling to my farm
I take little brown jug under my arm,
Place him under a shady tree—
Little brown jug, 'tis you and me.
Chorus

4. If I'd a cow that gave such milk,
I'd clothe her in the finest silk,
I'd feed her on the choicest hay,
And milk her forty times a day.
Chorus

5. The rose is red, my nose is, too.
The violet's blue and so are you;
And yet I guess, before I stop
I'd better take another drop.
Chorus

CHORUS

Ha! ha! ha! you and me,
Little brown jug, don't I love thee!
Ha! ha! ha! you and me,
Little brown jug, don't I love thee!

Tiritomba

A gay Neapolitan folk song brought over by the Italians, who were at this time coming to America in great numbers.

Moderato

English translation by Maria X. Hayes

mp *F* *F*

1. Se - ra jet - te, se - ra jet - te a la ma - ri - na, Pe tra-
1. I went out one pleas-ant eve-ning by the sea - shore, Just to

staccato

mp

Ped. ※ Ped. ※ Ped. ※

C7 F F

và 'na 'nna - mo - ra - ta, Jan-ca e ros - sa, jan-ca e ros-sa ag-gra - zi -
see if I could meet there With a maid-en fair and ros - y, young and

Ped. ※ Ped. ※ Ped. ※

F C7 F C7

a - ta, Fat-to pro - prio pe scia - là. Ti - ri - tom - ba, ti - ri-
sweet there, Made ex-act - ly to my mind. Ti - ri - tom - ba, ti - ri-

Ped. ※ Ped. ※ Ped. ※

200

tom - ba! Ti - ri - tom - ba, n'e lu ve - ro si o no? Ti - ri -
tom - ba! Ti - ri - tom - ba, is it true now, yes or no? Ti - ri -

tom - ba, Ti - ri - tom - ba! Ti - ri - tom - ba al - l'a - rià và!
tom - ba, ti - ri - tom - ba! Ti - ri - tom - ba, off we go!

2. Then as up and down, and here and there I wandered,
   Soon I heard a murmured sigh there.
   Then I turned, O, then I turned and drew more nigh there,
   As I paused and looked behind.
   Chorus

3. As I gazed and gazed again, she smiled upon me.
   Then I spoke; she answered sweetly,
   And that plunged me in a sea of love completely,
   And my heart was almost won.
   Chorus

4. When all suddenly, so suddenly before me,
   Her papa came quite ferocious,
   With a weighty stick and language quite atrocious,
   Ev'ry bone he vowed he'd break.
   Chorus

5. How I scampered, how I scurried, how I hurried,
   From his blows so dreadful flying;
   But by night and day for that fair girl I'm sighing,
   Whom I never shall forget.
   Chorus

CHORUS

Tiritomba, tiritomba!
Tiritomba, is it true now, yes or no?
Tiritomba, tiritomba!
Tiritomba, off we go!

The Big Sunflower

*"The Big Sunflower," the theme song of Billy Emerson
(William Emerson Redmond) one of the greatest of
minstrels, was a favorite number in minstrel shows.*

As sung by Billy Emerson

Allegro moderato

1. There is a charm I can't ex-plain, A-bout a girl I've
2. As days passed on and we be-came Like friends of old-en

202

From *Americans and Their Songs* by Frank Luther. By permission of Harper & Brothers, publishers.

seen; My heart beats fast when she goes past In a dress all trimmed with
times, I thought the ques-tion I would pop, And ask her to be

green; Her eyes are bright as eve-ning stars, So lov-ing and so
mine, But the an-swer I re-ceived next day,—How could she treat me

shy, And the folks all stop and look a-round When-ev-er she goes by.
so? In - stead of be - ing mine for life, She sim-ply an-swered "No."

Chorus

And I feel just as hap-py as a big sun-flow'r, That

nods and bends in the breez - es; And my heart is as light as the

wind that blows the__ leaves from off the trees - es.

3. I went next day dressed in my best,
This young girl for to see,
To ask her if she would explain
Why she had shaken me.
She said she really felt quite sad
To cause me such distress,
And when I said: "Won't you be mine?"
Of course she answered: "Yes."

CHORUS

And I feel just as happy as a big sunflower
That nods and bends in the breezes;
And my heart's as light as the wind that blows
The leaves from off the trees-es.

Oh, Dem Golden Slippers!

James Bland, well-known minstrel and song writer, wrote most of his songs, as did Stephen Foster, for immediate use in minstrel shows. "Oh, Dem Golden Slippers," with its carefree, humorous warmth, was highly successful in the 80's and still is one of our most popular songs.

Words and Music by James A. Bland

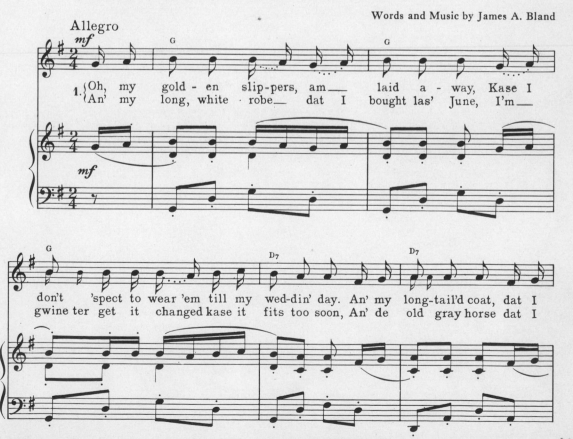

1. Oh, my gold-en slip-pers, am laid a-way, Kase I
   An' my long, white robe dat I bought las' June, I'm

don't 'spect to wear 'em till my wed-din' day. An' my long-tail'd coat, dat I
gwine ter get it changed kase it fits too soon, An' de old gray horse dat I

Gold-en slip-pers I'm gwine ter wear, to walk de gold-en streets.

2. Oh, my old banjo hangs on de wall,
Kase it ain't been tuned since way las' fall.
But de darkies all say we will have a good time,
When we ride up in de chariot in de morn.
Dere's old Brother Ben an' Sister Luce,
Dey will telegraph de news to Uncle 'Bacco Juice,
What a great camp meetin' dere will be dat day,
When we ride up in de chariot in de morn.
Chorus

3. Good-by, children, I will have to go,
Where de rain don't fall or de wind don't blow,
An' yo' ulster coats, why, you will not need,
When you ride up in de chariot in de morn.
But de golden slippers mus' be neat an' clean,
An' yo' age mus' be jes' sweet sixteen,
An' yo' white kid gloves you will have to wear,
When you ride up in de chariot in de morn.
Chorus

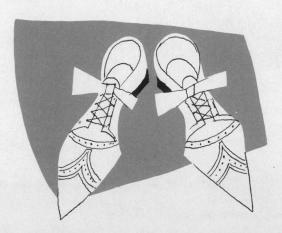

CHORUS

Oh, dem golden slippers! Oh, dem golden slippers!
Golden slippers I'm gwine ter wear, because dey look so neat;
Oh, dem golden slippers! Oh, dem golden slippers!
Golden slippers I'm gwine ter wear, to walk de golden streets.

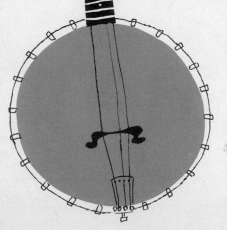

207

The Wabash Cannon Ball

*When railroads spread over the whole country and completed the opening
of the West, the train became a symbol of freedom—freedom to move about
at will. People sang of its speed, its noise, its rhythm, and of
the changes it would make in their lives.*

Words and Music by Roger Truhart

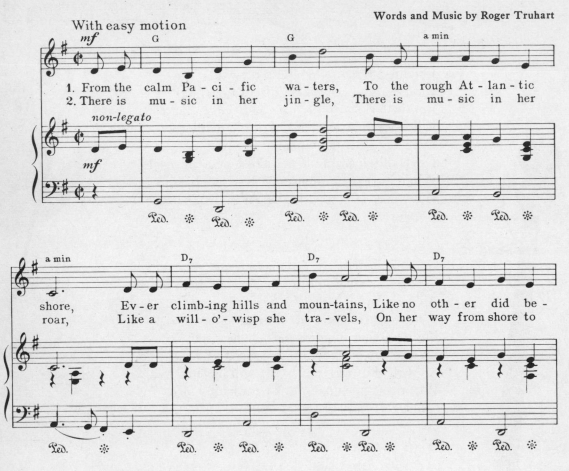

With easy motion

1. From the calm Pa - ci - fic wa - ters, To the rough At - lan - tic
2. There is mu - sic in her jin - gle, There is mu - sic in her

shore, Ev - er climb-ing hills and moun-tains, Like no oth - er did be -
roar, Like a will - o'- wisp she tra - vels, On her way from shore to

The Wabash Cannon Ball

fore. / shore. She's as grace-ful as a com-et, Smooth-er than a wa-ter / May her great-ness last for - ev - er, May the glo-ry nev-er

fall, / fail, It's the West-ern Com-bi - na-tion, It's the Wa-bash Can-non Ball. / Of the West-ern Com-bi - na-tion, Of the Wa-bash Can-non Ball.

Take This Hammer

A Negro work song. The job of the steel driver was one of the most dangerous and gruelling of all railroad construction jobs. The men took pride in their prowess with the hammer, and as they drilled into the rock for blasting charges they often sang boastingly of their strength, their endurance, and sometimes of their indignation against the boss.

Words and Melody adapted and arranged by John A. and Alan Lomax

With energy

1. Take this ham - mer, (Huh!) Car-ry it to the cap - tain,
2. If he asks you (Huh!) Was I run - ning,

From *Our Singing Country*, compiled and copyrighted by John A. and Alan Lomax.

3. If he asks you was I laughing *(3 times)*
   Tell him I was crying, tell him I was crying.

4. I don't want no cornbread and molasses, *(3 times)*
   They hurt my pride, they hurt my pride.

5. I don't want no cold iron shackles *(3 times)*
   Around my leg, around my leg.

The Streets of Laredo

*Alan Lomax considers this story of the ruined young cowboy the
most popular Western ballad after "The Old Chisholm Trail."*

Words and Melody adapted and arranged by John A. and Alan Lomax

1. As I_____ walked out in the streets of La-re-do, As
I walked out in La-re-do one day, I spied a dear cow-boy wrapped up in white lin-en Wrapped

2. "I see by your out-fit that you are a cow-boy"—These
words he did say as I bold-ly stepped by, "Come sit down be-side me and hear my sad sto-ry; I am

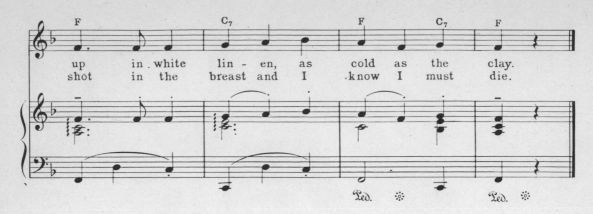

up   in white   lin - en,   as   cold   as   the   clay.
shot   in the   breast and   I   know   I   must   die.

3. "It was once in the saddle I used to go dashing,
    It was once in the saddle I used to go gay;
    First to the dram-house and then to the card-house;
    Got shot in the breast and I am dying today.

4. "Oh, beat the drum slowly and play the fife lowly,
    Play the dead march as you carry me along;
    Take me to the green valley, there lay the sod o'er me,
    For I'm a young cowboy and I know I've done wrong.

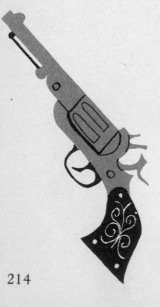

5. "Get six jolly cowboys to carry my coffin;
    Get six pretty maidens to bear up my pall.
    Put bunches of roses all over my coffin,
    Put roses to deaden the sods as they fall.

6. "Then swing your rope slowly and rattle your spurs lowly,
    And give a wild whoop as you carry me along;
    And in the grave throw me and roll the sod o'er me,
    For I'm a young cowboy and I know I've done wrong.

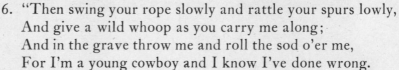

7. "Go bring me a cup, a cup of cold water,
    To cool my parched lips," the cowboy then said.
    Before I returned, his soul had departed
    And gone to the round-up—the cowboy was dead.

8. We beat the drum slowly and played the fife lowly,
    And bitterly wept as we bore him along;
    For we all loved our comrade, so brave, young, and handsome,
    We all loved our comrade although he'd done wrong.

Eight Hours

The campaign for an eight-hour work day, begun in earnest after the Civil War, resulted in the passage of an eight-hour law by Congress on June 25, 1868. It proved ineffectual. Blanchard's song, written during the original campaign, was revived in the 80's, when labor worked for a more effective law. It became the official song of the movement, which culminated in a great demonstration on May 1, 1886—the first May Day celebration. The song is rendered here as sung by Wally Hille.

Words by I. G. Blanchard

Music by Rev. Jesse H. Jones

1. We mean to make things o - ver, we are tired of toil for naught, With but bare e-nough to live up-on and ne'er an hour for thought;— We want to feel the sun-shine, and we want to smell the

2. The beasts that graze the hill-side, and the birds that wan-der free, In the life that God has me - ted, have a bet - ter life than we.— Oh, hands and hearts are wea - ry, and homes are heav-y with

215

flow'rs, We are sure that God has willed it, and we mean to have eight

dole; If our life's to be filled with drudg-'ry, what need of a hu-man

hours. We're sum-mon-ing our for-ces from the ship-yard, shop, and mill.

soul! Shout, shout the lust-y ral-ly from the ship-yard, shop, and mill.

Chorus

Eight hours for work, eight hours for rest,

Eight hours for what we will, Eight hours for

work, eight hours for rest, Eight hours for what we will.

3. The voice of God within us is calling us to stand
Erect as is becoming to the work of His right hand.
Should he, to whom the Maker His glorious image gave,
The meanest of His creatures crouch, a bread-and-butter slave?
Let the shout ring down the valleys and echo from every hill.
Chorus

4. Ye deem they're feeble voices that are raised in labor's cause?
But bethink ye of the torrent, and the wild tornado's laws.
We say not toil's uprising in terror's shape will come,
Yet the world were wise to listen to the momentary hum.
Soon, soon, the deep-toned rally shall all the nations thrill.
Chorus

5. From factories and workshops in long and weary lines,
From all the sweltering forges, and from out the sunless mines,
Wherever toil is wasting the force of life to live,
There the bent and battered armies come to claim what God doth give,
And the blazon on the banner doth with hope the nation fill.
Chorus

6. Hurrah, hurrah, for labor, for it shall arise in might.
It has filled the world with plenty, it shall fill the world with light.
Hurrah, hurrah, for labor, it is mustering all its powers
And shall march along to victory with the banner of eight hours.
Shout, shout the echoing rally till all the welkin thrill.
Chorus

CHORUS

Eight hours for work, eight hours for rest,
Eight hours for what we will.
Eight hours for work, eight hours for rest,
Eight hours for what we will.

The Old Chisholm Trail

The Old Chisholm Trail was the main highway from Texas, the best breeding ground for cattle, to Kansas, the nearest shipping point to the markets. Half-wild longhorns were driven over it by the thousands each year. The long drive up the trail occupied months, and each trip added new stanzas to the cowboys' favorite song,
"The Old Chisholm Trail."

Words and Melody adapted and arranged by John A. and Alan Lomax

1. Come a - long,— boys, and lis - ten to my tale, I'll
started up the trail, Oc - to - ber twen - ty - third, I

tell you of my trou - bles on the old Chis-holm Trail. Com - a
start - ed up the trail— with the 2 - U— herd.

ti - yi youp-y, youp-y yea, youp-y yea, Com-a

ti yi youp-y, youp-y yea. 2. I

3. O a ten-dollar hoss and a forty-dollar saddle,
   And I'm goin' to punch in Texas cattle.
   Chorus

4. I woke up one morning on the old Chisholm trail,
   Rope in my hand and a cow by the tail.
   Chorus

5. Stray in the herd and the boss said to kill it,
   So I shot him in the rump with the handle of the skillet.
   Chorus

6. My hoss throwed me off at the creek called Mud,
   My hoss throwed me off round the 2-U herd.
   Chorus

7. Last time I saw him he was going 'cross the level
   A-kicking up his heels and a-running like the devil.
   Chorus

8. It's cloudy in the west, a-looking like rain,
   And my damned old slicker's in the wagon again.
   Chorus

9. The wind commenced to blow and the rain began to fall.
   Hit looked, by grab, like we was goin' to lose 'em all.
   Chorus

10. I jumped in the saddle, grabbed holt of the horn—
    Best damned cowpuncher ever was born.
    Chorus

11. I popped my foot in the stirrup and gave a little yell.
    The tail cattle broke and the leaders went to hell.
    Chorus

12. Feet in the stirrups and seat in the saddle,
    I hung and rattled with them goddamn cattle.
    Chorus

13. I don't give a damn if they never do stop,
    I'll ride as long as an eight-day clock.
    Chorus

14. We rounded 'em up and put 'em on the cars,
    And that was the last of the old Two Bars.
    Chorus

15. Goin' to the boss to git my money,
    Goin' back south to see my honey.
    Chorus

16. With my hand on the horn and my seat in the sky,
    I'll quit herding cows in the sweet by-and-by.
    Chorus

CHORUS

Coma ti yi youpy, youpy yea, youpy yea,
Coma ti yi youpy, youpy yea.

221

The Jam on Gerry's Rocks

This is one of the best known and most widely sung of the lumberjack songs—
one of the few, according to Stewart Holbrook, to reach the Pacific Coast
camps. It describes death by the log jam, perhaps the biggest
and most spectacular hazard in lumbering.

Sadly, but with motion

1. Come all ye jo-vial shant-y boys, Wher-ev-er you may be, I
hope you'll pay at-ten-tion, And lis-ten un-to me; Con-
cern-ing six brave shant-y boys With courage strong and brave, Who

2. 'Twas on one Sun-day morn-ing In the spring-time of the year, Our
logs were pil-ing moun-tain high, We could not keep them clear; When our
boss, he cried: "Brave boys, turn out, Set your hearts, a-void all fear, We'll

From E. H. Linscott, *Folk Songs of Old New England*, copyright 1939 by The Macmillan Co., and used with their permission.

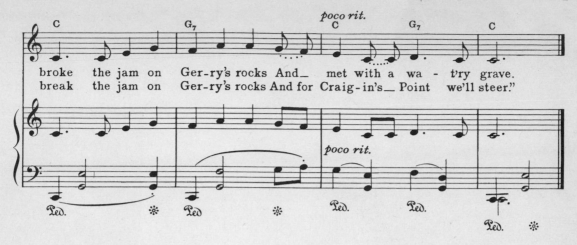

broke   the jam on   Ger-ry's rocks And—   met with a wa - t'ry grave.
break   the jam on   Ger-ry's rocks And for Craig-in's— Point we'll steer."

poco rit.

3. Now some of them were willing,
   While others did hang back,
   For to go to work on Sunday
   They did not think it right.
   When six Canadian shanty boys
   Did volunteer to go,
   To break the jam on Gerry's rocks
   With the foreman, young Monroe.

4. Now they had not rolled off many logs
   When the boss to them did say,
   "I'd have you be on your guard;
   This jam will soon give way."
   He had no more than spoke those words
   When the jam did heave and go
   And carried away those six brave youths
   And their foreman, young Monroe.

5. Now when their comrades at the camp
   The sad news came to hear,
   In search of their dead bodies
   Down the river they did steer.
   When to their sad misfortune,
   To their sad grief and woe,
   All bruised and mangled on the beach
   Lies the head of young Monroe.

6. We picked it up most carefully,
   Smoothed down his raven hair.
   There was one fair form among them
   Whose cries would rend the air.
   There was one fair form among them,
   A girl from Sag'mor town,
   Whose screams and cries would rend the skies,
   For her true love was drowned.

7. His mother was a widow,
   Near by the river side.
   Miss Clark she was a very nice girl
   And his intended bride.
   The money that was due to him
   The boss to her did pay;
   She received a large subscription
   From the shanty boys next day.

8. We buried him quite decently,
   Being on the sixth of May.
   Come, all you jovial shanty boys,
   And for your comrade pray;
   For engraved upon a hemlock tree,
   Which on the beach did grow,
   The day, the date, and the drowning fate
   Of our comrade, young Monroe.

Jesse James

In 1882 Jesse James, famous bandit and train robber, was living in hiding in St. Joseph, Missouri, under the name of Howard. Tempted by the reward offered for Jesse James, Robert Ford, a member of his gang and supposedly a friend, shot him in the back while he was hanging a picture on the wall of his home.

Not too fast

1. Jes-se James was a lad who___ killed man-y a man. He___
2. It was Rob-ert___ Ford, that___ dirt-y lit-tle cow-ard; I___

From *A Treasury of American Song* by Olin Downes and Elie Siegmeister, published by Alfred A. Knopf, Inc., copyright 1943.

robbed the Glen-dale_ train. He_ stole from the rich and he
won - der how he does feel, For he ate of Jes - se's bread and he

gave_ to the poor; He'd a hand and a heart and a brain.
slept in Jes-se's bed, Then laid poor Jes - se in his grave. Poor

Jes - se had a wife to_ mourn for his life; Three chil - dren, they were

brave; But that dirt - y lit - tle cow - ard_ that

shot Mis- ter How- ard__ Has laid poor__ Jes- se in his grave.

3. Jesse was a man, a friend to the poor;
   He never would see a man suffer pain;
   And with his brother Frank he robbed the Chicago bank,
   And stopped the Glendale train.
   Chorus

4. It was on Saturday night; Jesse was at home
   Talking with his family brave.
   Robert Ford came along like a thief in the night
   And laid poor Jesse in his grave.
   Chorus

5. This song was made by Billy Gashade,
   As soon as the news did arrive;
   He said there was no man with the law in his hand
   Who could take Jesse James when alive.
   Chorus

CHORUS

Poor Jesse had a wife to mourn for his life;
Three children, they were brave;
But that dirty little coward that shot Mister Howard
Has laid poor Jesse in his grave.

White Wings

*"White Wings," a popular novel of the 80's by William
Black, furnished the title and subject matter for Banks
Winter's famous song. "White Wings" refers to the sails
of a ship, and the story is of a sailor, hurrying
home to his bride.*

Words and Music by Banks Winter

Sail! home as straight as an ar-row, My yacht shoots a-long on the
crest of the sea; Sail! home, to sweet Mag-gie Dar-row, In her
dear lit-tle home she is wait-ing for me. High up! where

car - ry me cheer-i — ly o - ver the sea; Night comes, I long for my dear-ie, I'll spread out my "White Wings" and sail home to thee!

Silver Threads among the Gold

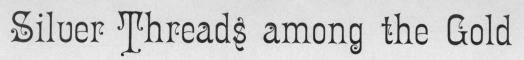

In the 70's, Hart P. Danks bought a batch of poems by Eben Rexford, the editor of a Wisconsin farm magazine, for three dollars each. One of these was "Silver Threads Among the Gold." Moved by the sentiment of the poem, Danks wrote a melody for it; this is sentimental, too, with a haunting wistfulness which endears it to around-the-piano singers now as it did two generations ago.

Words by Eben E. Rexford

Music by H. P. Danks

With sentiment

1. Dar - ling, I am grow - ing old, Sil - ver threads a-mong the gold, Shine up-on my brow to-day; Life is fad-ing fast a - way;
2. When your hair is sil - ver white, And your cheeks no long-er bright, With the ros - es of the May, I will kiss your lips and say:

232

Sil - ver threads a-mong the gold. Shine up-on my brow to-

day; Life is fad-ing fast a - way.

3. Love can never more grow old.
   Locks may lose their brown and gold,
   Cheeks may fade and hollow grow,
   But the hearts that love will know
   Never, never, winter's frost and chill,
   Summer warmth is in them still;
   Never winter's frost and chill,
   Summer warmth is in them still.

4. Love is always young and fair.
   What to us is silver hair,
   Faded cheeks or steps grown slow,
   To the heart that beats below?
   Since I kissed you, mine alone, alone,
   You have never older grown;
   Since I kissed you, mine alone,
   You have never older grown.

CHORUS

Darling, I am growing old;
Silver threads among the gold
Shine upon my brow today;
Life is fading fast away.

Independence—On to the West

FROM 1776

THE SONGS of this period are the songs of a new nation. And in one form or another they are songs of rebellion, for the American colonists were a rebellious breed. They fought a great revolution because they would not tolerate the English rule, and after the Revolution they continued to fight with each other. Their religion underwent drastic reformations; and finally, in a great surge of the independent spirit, they spread out and peopled the whole vast continent which is now the United States.

Nothing shows the fiery spirit of the colonists as well as the songs they sang. Political organization was the great preoccupation. The American Whigs were organizing a war for independence. England's misguided attempts to tax the colonies, to quarter British soldiers in them at American expense, had infuriated almost everybody. It was easy for the Sons of Liberty to whip up public feeling: there was mob violence; the Boston massacre particularly caught the imagination of a still disunited nation; and there were the songs. They were printed on broadsheets and distributed everywhere. Parodies of famous old English tunes, hymns, parodies of parodies—they were all designed to inflame. When in 1775 the "shot heard round the world" was fired, and the colonists were plunged into a six-year war of revolution, the songs went to war with them. "Yankee Doodle," "The Liberty Song," "Chester," and many others were on everybody's lips. It was a war to free Americans from political domination. Politics was the absorbing topic everywhere.

Victory did not end this preoccupation. During the Revolution, every American had felt himself the master of his own destiny. When it was over, his interest in the creation of the new country was intense, and the dissident spirit remained strong. The

Constitutional Convention met and drew up a Constitution. After public discussion it was adopted and amended. George Washington, the first President, was chosen with unanimity. But from then on the scene was set for political strife.

There was strife even against the Federal government which had united the states. In western Pennsylvania, farmers felt that they had a right to do what they pleased with their own crops, and the Whiskey Rebellion arose against Federal attempts to tax the liquor which they made—a fight which Kentucky mountaineers have carried on right up to modern times.

Federalism as opposed to states' rights was the burning issue. It split the nation into two major parties, the Federalists and the Jeffersonian Democrats. Party feeling was so great when Great Britain went to war against France that Joseph Hopkinson wrote "Hail, Columbia" in an effort to arouse some kind of unity among Americans. But when the United States declared war against Britain in 1812, sentiment was still so divided that an enormous number of people were opposed to the fighting.

It was a half-hearted kind of war. We attacked Canada and burned Toronto; the British attacked and burned Washington. We had some brilliant naval victories, but we did not do so well on land. Two weeks after a treaty was signed in Europe, Andrew Jackson, in the battle of New Orleans, won our only great land victory, not having heard that the war was over.

Meantime, the same surge of self-assertion which made Americans such aggressive citizens was helping to create a native culture. Our first composers developed at about the time of the Revolution. They were a widely divergent group of men, ranging from the polished Hopkinson (who wrote "Enraptured I Gaze," and who was the friend of Washington, Jefferson, and Franklin, and a signer of the Declaration of Independence) to William Billings, the semi-illiterate ex-tanner who wrote "Chester" and many other famous hymns. Billings spent his whole life sponsoring a native American music. He was one of the first of the many music teachers who sprang up in the new states, establishing schools, generally in country taverns, and bringing music to whole communities which had been entirely cut off from it until then.

At this time the "shape note" songbooks appeared. These represented our first printed music and were designed by the rural music teachers to simplify the reading of music so that people with no education could learn to sing by note. "Shape notes" were crude symbols (triangles, circles, squares) arbitrarily indicating by their shapes the pitch to be sung, without regard to the lines and spaces on the staff. The innovation met with great opposition from the conservatives, one New England newspaper going so far as to say: "If we once begin to sing by note, the next thing will be to pray by rule and preach by rule, and then comes popery." But the books were vastly popular, particularly in backwoods communities, and some of them are still used in the rural South today.

Side by side with our struggles for political independence, the same old fight for religious freedom was continuing. Baptists, Methodists, and Congregationalists were multiplying, and dozens of dissident sects were splitting off from these. In the backwoods, where pioneers met on the same footing, sectarianism began to disappear in a new democracy of religion. The Kentucky Revival of 1800, which was the first of the camp-meeting revivals, held open house for all sects. The common bond among the people who attended was an hysterical frenzy, unheard of in earlier religious movements. Out of such camp meetings, and those inspired later by the Millenial Movement of 1830-43, the White spiritual was born. (Authorities disagree as to the origin of the spirituals and whether White or Negro spirituals came first.) It was a type of song to appeal to a mass of people, worked up to so great an emotional pitch that only the simplest and most direct form of singing would reach them. Strong rhythm, constant repetition, and a continuously reiterated chorus made these songs different from the folk hymns which until then had been the most liberal type of religious music sung.

No matter how earnestly Americans were preoccupied with politics and religion, they found time for frivolity too, increasingly so as the new country began to feel its oats in the exuberance of expansion. They sang the folk songs that immigrants had brought from their homelands. They developed an opera and a theatre. And in those communities where religious groups frowned on dancing, the play party was popular. Young people met at these parties to play singing games such as "Skip to My Lou" and "Pop! Goes the Weasel," and although they went all through the motions of clapping, stamping, kissing forfeits, and sometimes even jigging, the parties still avoided the stigma of dancing. The chief distinction was that no musical instrument was ever used, the entire accompaniment being vocal.

Another and even more purely native form of pleasure was developed in the early minstrel shows. This form of amusement came to its peak at a later period, but the first minstrel song, "Jump Jim Crow," was written about 1830 by Thomas Rice. In 1843 the original Big Four of Minstrelsy, Dan Emmett, Billy Whitlock, Dick Pelham, Frank Bromer, got together and started the Virginia Minstrels—a blackface show which opened at the Bowery Theatre in New York. It was immediately copied by other companies, and a new entertainment, which was to be popular for more than a century, was launched.

During all this time, America was expanding by leaps and bounds. The great logging and lumber industry which began long before the Revolution had reached a new peak. Lumbermen moved from New England to New York, to Pennsylvania, Michigan, and Wisconsin, as the demand grew for tall trees to build homes and ships. French-Canadian and American lumbermen worked from border to border and exchanged friendship and songs.

On the sea, great clipper ships brought spices, silks, and tea from the Orient; whaling boats ventured into many waters; passenger vessels crossed the ocean and rounded Cape Horn. It was the day of sailing ships and sea shanties.

On the land, Americans expanded westward. First they went in hunting, scouting, pioneer groups. Then as canals were built in the East and travel made easier, whole families of farmer citizens went in caravans to find permanent homes. The Erie Canal, about which so many songs have been written, opened up a passageway for New

England and New York. From the South, the Scotch-Irish moved West. The Germans of Pennsylvania made their way through the wilderness.

These pioneers developed into a new type of citizen—staunchly independent and utterly individualistic. The European traditions which clung to Americans of the East Coast were transformed in the West. Every man had equal opportunity, based not on his fortune or his birth, but on his abilities. These new Americans were often crude and, on the surface, unsentimental, and they made up a stalwart part of our country. Their songs are an excellent reflection of that sardonic, gaily independent spirit which became typical of the Westerner.

In fact, the entire picture of the Western movement can be told in the songs the pioneers sang. There are the hymns of the Mormons who moved West to escape religious persecution and made a garden out of the desert state of Utah. There are the Gold Rush songs, a cynical picture of that turbulent migration. Gold was discovered just as we signed the peace treaty with Mexico which gave us the whole territory of California. Nearly 300,000 Americans crowded into the gold fields within the next ten years. Farmers, lawyers, sailors, and newspapermen abandoned everything and went overland or around the Cape in ships to stake out their claims. It was one of the most adventurous and boisterous pages of our pioneering history.

And the vigorous songs of that day added one more page to the fiery, exuberant music of the era—the music of a new nation which saw no limits to expansion or to hope.

The Liberty Song

"The Liberty Song," the first American patriotic ballad, was written by John Dickinson, celebrated lawyer of Delaware. Its publication in 1768 began a battle of ballads between the patriots and the Tories. One of the most famous patriot retorts to a Tory parody on the final stanza of Dickinson's poem is printed below.

Words by John Dickinson   Tune: "Hearts of Oak" by William Boyce

1. Come, join hand in hand, brave A-mer-i-cans all, And rouse your bold hearts at fair Lib-er-ty's call; No tyr-an-nous acts shall sup-

2. Our wor-thy fore-fa-thers, let's give them a cheer, To cli-mates un-known did cou-ra-geous-ly steer; Thro' o-ceans to des-erts for

The Liberty Song

press your just claim, Or stain with dis-hon-or A-mer-i-ca's name.
Free-dom they came, And dy-ing, be-queath'd us their free-dom and fame.} In—

Free-dom we're born and in Free-dom we'll live. Our pur-ses are— read-y.

Stead-y, friends, stead-y, Not as slaves, but as Free-men our mon-ey we'll give.—

3. The tree their own hands had to Liberty rear'd,
They lived to behold growing strong and revered;
With transport they cried, "Now our wishes we gain,
For our children shall gather the fruits of our pain."
Chorus

4. Then join hand in hand, brave Americans all,
By uniting we stand, by dividing we fall;
In so righteous a cause let us hope to succeed,
For heaven approves of each generous deed.
Chorus

CHORUS

In Freedom we're born and in Freedom we'll live.
Our purses are ready,
Steady, friends, steady;
Not as slaves, but as Freemen our money we'll give.

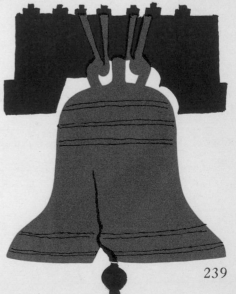

Yankee Doodle

This gay tune played an important part in the American Revolution. It is said to have been sung first by the British during the French and Indian War (1754-1763) in derision of the New England troops, and later by the British during the early part of the Revolution, again in derision of the Americans. But the Americans liked the tune and during the latter part of the Revolution took it from the enemy. The bands of the Continental Army played it, so it has been stated, when Cornwallis surrendered his army to Washington at Yorktown on October 19, 1781.

Fast and perkily

1. __ Fa - ther and I went down to camp, A - long with Cap - tain
2. And there was Cap - tain Wash - ing - ton Up - on a slap - ping

Good - ing, And there we saw the men and boys, As thick as hast - y pud - ding.
stal - lion, A - giv - ing or - ders to his men; I guess there were a mil - lion.

240

Chorus

Yan - kee Doo-dle, keep it up, Yan - kee Doo-dle dan - dy,

Mind the mu - sic and the step, And with the girls be han - dy.

3. The flaming ribbons in his hat,
   They look'd so tarnal fine, ah,
   I wanted pockily to get
   To give to my Jemimah.
   Chorus

4. And there they had a swampin' gun,
   As big as a log of maple,
   Upon a deuced little cart,
   A load for father's cattle.
   Chorus

5. And every time they fired it off
   It took a horn of powder;
   It made a noise like father's gun,
   Only a nation louder.
   Chorus

6. I went as nigh to it myself,
   As 'Siah's underpinnin',
   And father went as near again—
   I thought the deuce was in him.
   Chorus

7. And there I see a little keg;
   Its heads were made of leather,
   They knocked upon't with little sticks,
   To call the folks together.
   Chorus

8. And there they'd fife away like fun,
   And play on corn-stalk fiddles;
   And some had ribbons red as blood,
   All bound around their middles.
   Chorus

9. The troopers, too, would gallop up,
   And fire right in our faces;
   It scared me almost half to death,
   To see them run such races.
   Chorus

10. Old Uncle Sam come there to change
    Some pancakes and some onions
    For 'lasses-cakes to carry home
    To give his wife and young ones.
    Chorus

11. But I can't tell you half I see,
    They kept up such a smother;
    So I took my hat off, made a bow,
    And scampered home to mother.
    Chorus

CHORUS

Yankee Doodle, keep it up,
Yankee Doodle dandy,
Mind the music and the step,
And with the girls be handy.

Chester

William Billings was a tanner by trade, half blind and with one short leg. He knew very little about music, but having a great desire to bring music to the people, he spent most of his life teaching, organizing singing schools, and writing music. During the Revolution he wrote prolifically and with burning patriotism. No song was more popular at that time than his "Chester." Tired soldiers sang it around their campfires night after night. It became the song of the Revolution.

Words and Music by William Billings

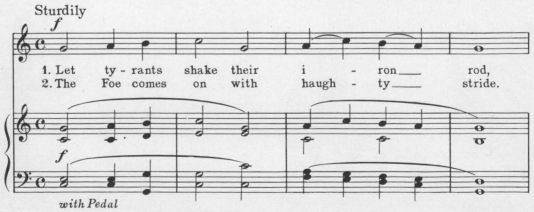

1. Let ty - rants shake their i - ron__ rod,
2. The Foe comes on with haugh - ty__ stride.

And Slav - 'ry clank her gall - - ing chains.
Our troops ad - vance with mar - - tial noise.

We fear them not; we trust in God,
Their Vet-'rans flee be - fore our Youth,

New Eng-land's God for - ev - - er reigns.
And Gen-'rals yield to beard - - less boys.

3. What grateful off'ring shall we bring?
What shall we render to this Lord?
Loud Hallelujah let us sing,
And praise His Name on ev'ry Chord.

Enraptured I Gaze

Francis Hopkinson, a charming musical amateur, a signer of the Declaration of Independence, and an intimate friend of Washington, was probably the earliest American composer of secular music. He seems to have been the center of musical life in Philadelphia, a musical life that for the first time extended into the home and was undisturbed by Quaker influences. "Enraptured I Gaze" is from the Set of Eight Songs *(1788), Hopkinson's most ambitious published work, which he dedicated to Washington.*

Words and Music by Francis Hopkinson

1. En - rap - tured I_____ gaze,___ when_ my_
2. I_____ hear_ her sweet_____ voice_ and_ am_

De - lia is_____ by, And drink the sweet___
charm'd_ with her_____ song I think I could_

poi - son of_____ love___ from her_ eye;___ I___
hear_ her sweet_ voice___ all day_ long; My_

244

3. Beyond all expression my Delia I love;
   My heart is so fix'd that it never can rove;
   When I see her I think 'tis an angel I see,
   And the charms of her mind are a heav'n to me.

Whisky Johnnie

*The work songs of the sailors were an essential part of the seafaring life. "Whisky Johnnie"
is one of the oldest of the halyard shanties, used for the larger and heavier
tasks aboard ship, such as hoisting sail and catting the anchor.*

1. Whis-ky is the life of man, Whis-ky John-nie. Oh!
2. I'll drink whis-ky when I can, Whis-ky John-nie. I'll

whis-ky is the___ life of man, Whis-ky for my John-nie.
drink it out of an old tin can, Whis-ky for my John-nie.

3. Whisky gave me a broken nose,
   Whisky Johnnie.
   Whisky made me pawn my clothes,
   Whisky for my Johnnie.

4. Whisky drove me around Cape Horn,
   Whisky Johnnie.
   It was many a month when I was gone,
   Whisky for my Johnnie.

5. I thought I heard the old man say,
   Whisky Johnnie,
   "I'll treat my crew in a decent way,"
   Whisky for my Johnnie.

6. A glass of grog for every man,
   Whisky Johnnie,
   And a bottleful for the chanteyman,
   Whisky for my Johnnie.

246

From E. H. Linscott, *Folk Songs of Old New England*, copyright 1939 by The Macmillan Co. and used with their permission.

Botany Bay

In 1787 Botany Bay, an inlet on the coast of New South Wales, was the site of a penal colony. This colony was later transferred to Sydney, Australia. "The Convict's Song" is said to have been composed by a convict who was transported to Australia in the 1800's.

1. Fare - well   to old   Eng - land the   beau - ti - ful!_____   Fare -
2. It's_ sev - en long years   I   been   serv - ing,_____   It's

well   to my   old   pals as   well!_____   Fare - well   to   the
sev - en   I   got   for to   stay,_____   For   beat - in' a

247

From *Frontier Ballads* by Charles J. Finger, copyright 1927 by Doubleday & Co., Inc.

Botany Bay

Too - ral li   Roo - lal li   Lay!

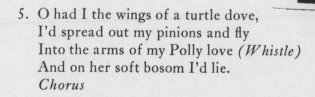

3. There's the captain what is our commandier,
   The bos'n an' all the ship's crew,
   The married and also the single ones *(Whistle)*
   Knows what us poor convicts goes through.
   Chorus

4. It ain't that they don't give us grub enough,
   It ain't that they don't give us clothes;
   It's all 'cause we light-fingered gentry *(Whistle)*
   Goes about with a chain on our toes.
   Chorus

5. O had I the wings of a turtle dove,
   I'd spread out my pinions and fly
   Into the arms of my Polly love *(Whistle)*
   And on her soft bosom I'd lie.
   Chorus

6. Now all you young viscounts and duchesses
   Take warning by what I do say,
   And mind it's all yours what you touches-es *(Whistle)*
   Or you'll land down in Botany Bay.
   Chorus

CHORUS

My
Too-ral li Roo-lal li Laity
Too-ral li Roo-lal li Lay
Too-ral li Roo-lal li Laity
Too-ral li Roo-lal li Lay!

The Oxen Song

Logging operations began in the American colonies in the 17th century. Oxen and horses were the first draft power in the woods. The crews were a mixture of Irish, French-Canadians, and Yankees, who went everywhere on tough and dangerous jobs. Their ballads reflect the proud, courageous spirit of the men.

Moderately fast

1. Come all you bold ox team-sters, Wher-ev-er you may be, I
2. It's of a bold ox team-ster, His name I'll tell to you, His

hope you'll pay at-ten-tion And lis-ten un-to me.
name was John-ny Car-pen-ter, He pulled the ox-en through.

3. 'Twas early in the season
In the fall of Twenty-five;
John Ross he sent four oxen up
For Carpenter to drive.

4. He took with him six bags of meal
And his bunk chains also,
All for to bind his spruce and pine
While hauling through the snow.

5. Says Carpenter unto Flemmons,
"I'll show them how to haul spruce,
For my oxen in the snow, you see,
Are equal to bull moose!"

6. Now the first day we was hauling
We landed forty-nine,
And in a short time after that
We began to fall behind.

7. Sebat he went to Carpenter,
These words to him did say:
"We've got to run another turn,
For this will never pay.

8. "We've got to run another turn,
And we'll all work together;
I've found a wonderful bunch of pine
'Way up at the head of the medder."

9. Now his oxen they have got so poor,
To haul they are not fit;
His sled looks like a butcher block,
All smeared with blood and grit.

10. He tried to keep his oxen fat,
But found it was no use;
For all that's left is skin and bones,
And all the horns are loose.

250

From E. H. Linscott, *Folk Songs of Old New England*, copyright 1939 by The Macmillan Co. and used with their permission.

Mister Banjo
[MONSIEUR BAINJO]

*A gay, satirical Creole song from Louisiana. The word "creole" is derived from the
Spanish word "criollo," meaning native to the locality.*

English Lyric by Joy Scott

Traditional English lyric by Joy Scott, arranged by Tom Scott, copyright 1946 by Joy Scott, from *Sing of America* by Tom Scott,
by permission of Thomas Y. Crowell Co., publishers, New York.

251

Old Colony Times

The original version of this ballad "may have preceded even the first attempts at colonization in our country; but the opening lines of this version, sung from Maine to Georgia, and at least as far west as Nebraska, were probably shaped around 1800, when 'old colony times' began to seem very remote." (From Series of Old American Songs, No. 41: S. Foster Damon)

1. In good old Col-o-ny times When we were un-der the king, Three ro-guish chaps fell
2. The first he was a mill-er, And the sec-ond he was a weav-er, And the third he was a

in - to mis-haps, Be - cause they could not sing.
lit - tle _ tail - or, Three ro - guish chaps to - geth - er. Be -

cause they could not sing, Be - cause they could not sing, Three

ro - guish chaps fell in - to mis-haps, Be - cause they could not sing.

3. Now the miller he stole corn
And the weaver he stole yarn
And the little tailor stole broadcloth for
To keep these three rogues warm.
Chorus

4. The miller got drown'd in his dam,
The weaver got hung in his yarn,
And the devil clapp'd his claw on the little tailor,
With the broadcloth under his arm.
Chorus

CHORUS
Because they could not sing,
Because they could not sing,
Three roguish chaps, fell into mishaps,
Because they could not sing.

253

The Pesky Sarpent

This is the first recorded American ballad and is founded on fact. Timothy Myrick, of Springfield, Massachusetts, was bitten by a rattlesnake on Friday, August 7, 1761, at Farmington, Massachusetts, and died before he could reach home. He was "very near the point of marriage" to Sarah Blake. The original ballad, an elegy on his tragic death, may have been sung at his funeral to the tune of "Old Hundredth," in accordance with a custom in western Massachusetts. Since then the song has traveled far and wide, has been given different dates and names, and has acquired many tunes.

1. On Springfield mountain there did dwell A comely youth I knew full well, Ri tu di na ri tu di na, Ri tu di na ri tu di na.

2. One Monday morning he did go Down in the meadow for to mow,

3. He scarce had mowed half the field,
   When a pesky sarpent bit his heel. Ri tu, etc.

4. He took his scythe and with a blow,
   He laid the pesky sarpent low. Ri tu, etc.

5. He took the sarpent in his hand,
   And straightway went to Molly Bland. Ri tu, etc.

6. Oh, Molly, Molly, here you see
   The pesky sarpent what bit me. Ri tu, etc.

7. Now Molly had a ruby lip,
   With which pizen she did sip. Ri tu, etc.

8. But Molly had a rotten tooth,
   Which the pizen struck and kill'd 'em both. Ri tu, etc.

9. The neighbors found that they were dead,
   So laid them both upon one bed. Ri tu, etc.

10. And all their friends both far and near
    Did cry and howl, they were so dear. Ri tu, etc.

11. Now all you maids a warning take
    From Molly Bland and Tommy Blake. Ri tu, etc.

12. And mind, when you're in love, don't pass
    Too near to patches of high grass. Ri tu, etc.

Bound for the Promised Land

Hundreds of stirring Hallelujah songs were born in the Great Revival that swept through Virginia, Kentucky, and Tennessee in the early 1800's. "Bound for the Promised Land," which traveled perhaps farthest of all these songs, reflects the optimism of a pioneer people and the courage of a young and growing country.

1. On Jor-dan's storm-y banks I stand And cast a wish-ful eye To Ca-naan's fair and hap-py land, Where my pos-ses-sions

2. O the trans-port-ing rap-t'rous scene That ris-es to my sight, Sweet fields ar-rayed in liv-ing green And rivers of de-

Juanita

The early Spanish families who came to California lived a simple and relatively easy life. There was
little to fear from the Indians; food was plentiful; there was time for love and laughter and singing.
Their songs reflecting this happiness have a soft rhythmical beauty and a gaiety not found
at that time in the songs from any other section of our country.

Tenderly

English words by Mrs. J. G. Norton

1. Cae la___ tar-de, len-ta-men-te so-bre el mar;
1. Soft o'er the foun-tain, Lin-g'ring falls the south-ern moon;

Tiem-blan las ho-jas del vas-to pi-nar.
Far o'er the moun-tain, Breaks the day too soon.

A-llá en la mon-ta-na se o-ye voz de un pas-tor,___
In thy dark eyes splen-dor, Where the warm light loves to dwell,___

259

2. When, in thy dreaming,
Moons like these shall shine again,
And, daylight beaming,
Prove thy dreams are vain,
Wilt thou not, relenting,
For thine absent lover sigh?
In thy heart consenting
To a prayer gone by!

CHORUS
Nita! Juanita!
Ask thy soul if we should part.
Nita! Juanita!
Lean thou on my heart.

Roll, Jordan, Roll

A beautiful version of this well-known spiritual.

1. O broth-ers,
2. O sis-ters,
3. O seek-ers,

you ought t'have been there, Yes, my Lord, A-sit-ting in the King-dom To hear Jor-dan roll.

Roll, Jor-dan, roll, Roll, Jor-dan, roll; I want to go to Heav-en when I die To hear Jor-dan roll.

Old Ship of Zion

One of the most primitive and most popular of the revival spirituals. This "White" version is said to have been written by Reverend Samuel Hauser, of North Carolina, in about 1800.

Melody transcribed by George Pullen Jackson

1. What ship is this that will take us all
   And safe-ly land us on Can-aan's bright

   home?
   shores? O glo-ry hal-le-lu-jah!

Old Ship of Zion

Chorus

'Tis the old ship of Zi-on, hal-le-lu, hal-le-lu, 'Tis the old ship of Zi-on, hal-le-lu - - jah!

2. The winds may blow and the billows may foam,
   O glory hallelujah!
   But she is able to land us all home.
   O glory hallelujah!
   Chorus

3. She's landed all who've gone before,
   O glory hallelujah!
   And yet she's able to land still more.
   O glory hallelujah!
   Chorus

4. If I arrive there before you do,
   O glory hallelujah!
   I'll tell them that you are coming up too.
   O glory hallelujah!
   Chorus

CHORUS
'Tis the old ship of Zion, hallelu, hallelu,
'Tis the old ship of Zion, hallelujah.

Were You There?

*The text of this spiritual had been current for more than a
century before it was set down in print. According to
George Pullen Jackson, a Negro-sung version
was the first to be transcribed.*

1. Were you there when they cru - ci - fied my Lord? _____
2. Were you there when they nailed Him to the tree? _____

Were you there when they cru - ci - fied my Lord?
Were you there when they nailed Him to the tree? } Oh, _____

264

From *The Book of American Negro Spirituals* by James Weldon Johnson and J. Rosamond Johnson,
published by The Viking Press, Inc., New York.

some-times it caus-es me to trem-ble, trem-ble, trem-ble; Were you

there when they cru - ci - fied my Lord? _____
there when they nailed Him to the tree? _____

3. Were you there when they pierced Him in the side?
Were you there when they pierced Him in the side?
O sometimes it causes me to tremble, tremble, tremble;
Were you there when they pierced Him in the side?

4. Were you there when the sun refused to shine?
Were you there when the sun refused to shine?
O sometimes it causes me to tremble, tremble, tremble;
Were you there when the sun refused to shine?

5. Were you there when they laid Him in the tomb?
Were you there when they laid Him in the tomb?
O sometimes it causes me to tremble, tremble, tremble;
Were you there when they laid Him in the tomb?

Hail, Columbia

Words by Joseph Hopkinson

Music by Philip Phile

1. Hail, Co-lum-bia, hap-py land, Hail, ye he - roes, heav'n born band, Who
2. Im-mor-tal pa-triots, rise once more, De-fend your rights, de - fend your shore, Let

"The President's March," one of the few tunes of lasting popularity associated with George Washington, is said to have been played for the first time as Washington ferried across the Delaware to Trenton on his way to New York for his inauguration ceremonies. In 1798 Gilbert Fox, a singer, asked Joseph Hopkinson to write a new patriotic song to that popular tune for him to use at a benefit. Hopkinson wrote "Hail, Columbia," which was immediately received with tremendous enthusiasm.

fought and bled in Free-dom's cause, Who fought and bled in Free-dom's cause, And
no rude foe with im - pi-ous hand, Let no rude foe with im - pi-ous hand, In-

Hail, Columbia

when the storm of war was gone, En - joy'd the peace your val - or won. Let
vade the shrine where sa - cred lies Of toil and blood the well earned prize, While

in - de - pen-dence be our boast, Ev - er mind-ful what it cost,
of - f'ring peace, sin - cere and just, In heav'n we place a man - ly trust, That

Ev - er grate-ful for the prize, Let its al - tar reach the skies.
truth and jus - tice may pre - vail, And ev - 'ry scheme of bond - age fail.

Chorus

Firm, u-nit-ed let us be, Ral-'ying round our lib-er-ty,

As a band of broth-ers join'd, Peace and safe-ty we shall find.

3. Sound, sound the trump of fame,
Let Washington's great fame
Ring through the world with loud applause,
Ring through the world with loud applause,
Let ev'ry chime to freedom dear,
Listen with a joyful ear,
With equal skill, with God-like pow'r
He governs in the fearful hour
Of horrid war, or guides with ease
The happier time of honest peace.
Chorus

4. Beloved the chief who now commands,
Once more to serve his country stands,
The rock on which the storm will beat,
The rock on which the storm will beat.
But arm'd in virtue firm and true,
His hopes are fixed on Heav'n and you,
When hope was sinking in dismay,
When glooms obscured Columbia's day,
His steady mind from changes free
Resolv'd on Death or Liberty.
Chorus

CHORUS

Firm united let us be,
Ral'ying round our liberty,
As a band of brothers joined,
Peace and safety we shall find.

269

Ye Parliament of England

A good account—from the American point of
view—of the naval battles of the War of 1812.

Words and Melody adapted and arranged by Joanna Colcord

Allegro
mf

1. Ye Par - lia - ment of Eng - land, Ye Lords and Com - mons too,— Con-
2. You first con - fined our com - merce, And said our ships shan't trade, You

non-legato

sid - er well what you're a - bout, What you're a - bout to do,— For
next im - pressed our sea - men, And used them as your slaves,— You

you're to war with Yan - kees, And I'm sure you'll rue the day— You
then in - sult - ed Rod - gers, While ply - ing o'er the main,— And

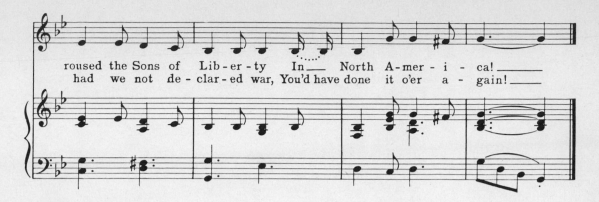

roused the Sons of Lib - er - ty In___ North A - mer - i - ca!___
had we not de - clar - ed war, You'd have done it o'er a - gain!___

3. You tho't our frigates were but few,
   And Yankees could not fight,
   Until brave HULL your GUERRIERE took
   And banished her from your sight.
   The WASP then took your FROLIC,
   We'll nothing say to that;
   The POICTIERS being of the line,
   Of course she took her back.

4. The next, your MACEDONIAN,
   No finer ship could swim,
   Decatur took her gilt work off,
   And then he sent her in.
   The JAVA by a Yankee ship
   Was sunk, you all must know;
   The PEACOCK fine, in all her plume,
   By Lawrence town did go.

6. The next upon Lake Erie,
   Where Perry had some fun,
   You own he beat your naval force
   And caused them for to run;
   This was to you a sore defeat,
   The like ne'er known before—
   Your British squadron beat complete—
   Some took, some run ashore.

5. Then, next you sent your BOXER,
   To box us all about,
   But we had an ENTERPRISING brig
   That boxed your BOXER out;
   She boxed her up to Portland,
   And moored her off the town,
   To show the sons of liberty
   The BOXER of renown.

7. There's Rodgers, in the PRESIDENT,
   Will burn, sink, and destroy;
   The CONGRESS, on the Brazil coast,
   Your commerce will annoy;
   The ESSEX, in the South Seas,
   Will put out all your lights;
   The flag she waves at her mast-head—
   "Free Trade and Sailor's Rights."

The Star Spangled Banner

With spirit, not too slow

Words by Francis Scott Key

1. Oh,— say can you see, by the dawn's ear-ly light, What so proud-ly we
2. On the shore dim-ly seen through the mist of the deep, Where the foe's haugh-ty
3. Oh,— thus be it ev - er, when free-men shall stand Be - tween their loved

hailed at the twi-light's last gleam-ing? Whose broad stripes and bright stars, thro' the
host in dread si - lence re - pos - es, What is that which the breeze, o'er the
homes and the war's des - o - la - tion, Blessed with vic - t'ry and peace, may the

per - il - ous fight, O'er the ram-parts we watched were so gal-lant-ly
tow - er - ing steep, As it fit - ful-ly blows, half con - ceals, half dis -
heav'n res-cued land Praise the pow'r that hath made and pre-served us a

272

Our national anthem was written by Francis Scott Key during the attack of the British on Fort McHenry, September 13, 1814. Key had gone out from Baltimore under a flag of truce to the British fleet to obtain the release of a friend held prisoner. He arrived on the eve of the bombardment of the city by the British and was detained lest the plans of the attack be disclosed. All day and night he watched the battle anxiously from the deck of his ship. When morning dawned and showed the Stars and Stripes still floating over the fort, he was deeply moved and began to write the words of the poem. It was later completed and set to the tune of an old English song, "Anacreon in Heaven," a tune which had been sung in this country for many years.

273

Darlin' Corey

"For toughness, for heroism, for pure cussedness, there are women in American folk-lore who can keep right up with their men. . . . There was the frontier type, the breed from which darling Corey, as a Kentucky moonshining gal, is derived." (John and Alan Lomax: Folksong U.S.A.)

Blues tempo   Words and Melody adapted and arranged by John A. and Alan Lomax

1. Wake up, wake up, dar-lin' Cor-ey,
2. The first time I saw dar-lin' Cor-ey,

What makes you
She was stand - - in'

sleep so sound? The
in the door. Her

Buckeye Jim

Fletcher Collins got this song from a friend in the hills of the Southern Appalachians. It has a quality of unreality, of mystery, quite unlike the feeling of other American songs about animals.

Transcribed by Fletcher Collins

Allegro moderato

1. Way up yon-der a - bove the moon, A Jay-bird lived in a sil - ver spoon.
2. Way up yon-der a - bove the sky, A Jay-bird built in a blue-bird's eye. } Go

lim-ber, Jim; you can't go. Go weave and spin, you can't go, Buck-eye Jim.

3. Way down yonder in a sycamore trough
   An old lady died with the whoopin'-cough.
   Go limber, Jim; you can't go.
   Go weave and spin, you can't go, Buckeye Jim.

4. Wake up snakes and come to taw,
   We won't have any more your link and law.
   Go limber, Jim; you can't go.
   Go weave and spin, you can't go, Buckeye Jim.

By permission of Fletcher Collins.

Pretty Saro

One of the most appealing of the songs expressing the social distinctions brought to the colonies from the old country.

1. Down in some lone valley in a lonesome place, Where the wild birds do whistle, and their notes do in-

2. My love she won't have me, so I understand, She wants a freeholder who owns house and

Pretty Saro

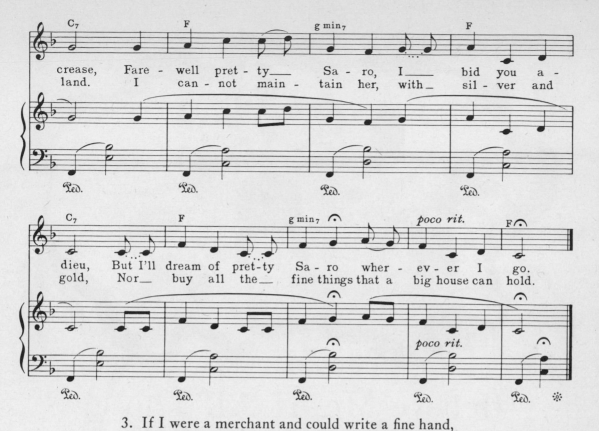

crease, Fare - well pret - ty__ Sa - ro, I__ bid you a -
land. I can - not main - tain her, with_ sil - ver and

dieu, But I'll dream of pret-ty Sa - ro wher - ev - er I go.
gold, Nor_ buy all the_ fine things that a big house can hold.

3. If I were a merchant and could write a fine hand,
   I'd write my love a letter that she'd understand;
   I'd write it by the river where the waters o'er-flow.
   And I'll dream of pretty Saro, wherever I go.

279

Believe Me, If All Those Endearing Young Charms

An Irish song of the early 1800's.

The E-RI-E

The Erie Canal, completed in 1825, became a great highway to the new states in the West. Barges loaded with merchandise were pulled by mules or horses, and life for the crews was easy, but slow. The "canaw-lers" often took to drink and singing to relieve the monotony of the trip.

Words and Melody adapted by John A. and Alan Lomax

1. We were for-ty miles from Al-ba-ny, For-get it, I nev-er shall. What a ter-ri-ble storm we had one night On the E-RI-E Ca-nal.
2. We were load-ed down with bar-ley, We were chock-up full of rye; And the cap-tain he looked down on me With a gol-durn wick-ed eye.

Chorus

O the E-RI-E was a-ris-in' And the

gin was a-git-tin' low, And I scarce-ly think we'll git a drink, Till we

get to Buf-fa - lo-o - o, Till we get to Buf-fa lo.

3. Two days out from Syracuse
   The vessel struck a shoal,
   And we like to all been foundered
   On a chunk o' Lackawanna coal.
   Chorus

4. We hollered to the captain
   On the towpath, treadin' dirt;
   He jumped on board and stopped the leak
   With his old red flannel shirt.
   Chorus

5. The cook she was a kind old soul,
   She had a ragged dress;
   We heisted her upon a pole
   As a signal of distress.
   Chorus

6. The winds begin to whistle
   And the waves begin to roll
   And we had to reef our royals
   On the raging Canawl.
   Chorus

7. When we got to Syracuse,
   The off-mule he was dead,
   The nigh mule got blind staggers
   And we cracked him on the head.
   Chorus

8. The captain, he got married,
   The cook, she went to jail,
   And I'm the only son-of-a-gun
   That's left to tell the tale.
   Chorus

CHORUS

O the E-RI-E was a-risin'
And the gin was a-gittin' low,
And I scarcely think we'll git a drink
Till we get to Buffa-lo-o-o,
Till we get to Buffalo.

Ye Banks and Braes

The tune was originally called "The Caledonian Hunt's Delight."
The words were written by Robert Burns in 1792.

Words by Robert Burns

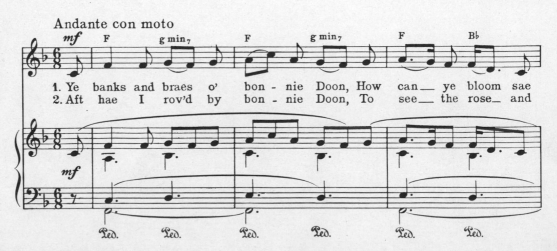

1. Ye banks and braes o' bon - nie Doon, How can__ ye bloom sae
2. Aft hae I rov'd by bon - nie Doon, To see__ the rose__ and

Wearin' of the Green

Not too fast

mf

1. Oh,—— Pad - dy, dear, and did ye hear the news that's go - in'
   Saint Pat-rick's day no more we'll keep, his col - or can't be

round? The sham-rock is for - bid by law to grow in I - rish ground!
seen, For there's a blood-y law a-gin' the wear-in' of the green!

I—— met with Nap - per Tan - dy, and he tuk me by the

hand, And he said, "How's poor old Ire - land, and how— does she stand?"

No one can place the authorship of this Irish song of 1798.
It is "an inspired street ballad born of the sorrow and the
bitterness of the people"—an eloquent arraignment
of England's Irish policy of the time.

She's the most dis-tress-ful coun-try__ that iv - er yet was seen, They're hang-in' men and wom-en there for wear-in' of the green.

2. An' if the color we must wear is England's cruel red,
   Sure Ireland's sons will ne'er forget the blood that they have shed.
   You may take the shamrock from your hat and cast it on the sod,
   But 'twill take root and flourish still, tho' underfoot 'tis trod.
   When laws can stop the blades of grass from growin' as they grow,
   And when the leaves in summertime their color dare not show,
   Then I will change the color, too, I wear in my caubeen,
   But 'till that day, plaze God, I'll stick to wearin' of the green.

3. But if at last our color should be torn from Ireland's heart,
   Her sons with shame and sorrow from the dear ould soil will part.
   I've heard whisper of a country that lies far beyant the say,
   Where rich and poor stand equal in the light of freedom's day.
   Oh, Erin! must we lave you, driven by the tyrant's hand,
   Must we ask a mother's welcome from a strange but happier land?
   Where the cruel cross of England's thraldom never shall be seen,
   And where, thank God, we'll live and die, still wearin' of the green.

287

Santy Anna

No one can explain why the facts in this popular shanty have been so twisted, nor why this particular Mexican general was so dear to the heart of the American sailor. When General Taylor defeated the Mexicans at Monterrey, in September 1846, Santa Anna, just returned from exile, was miles away in Mexico City. In February 22-23, 1847, Santa Anna met General Taylor for the first time, at Buena Vista, and was defeated.

Words and Melody adapted and arranged by Joanna Colcord

1. O Santy Anna gained the day, Hoo-
2. And Gen-'ral Tay-lor ran a-way,

ray, Santy Anna! He lost it once but
He ran a-way at

gained it twice, All on the plains of Mex-i-co!
Mon-te-rey,

288

3. Oh, Santy Anna fought for fame,
   Hooray, Santy Anna!
   And there's where Santy gained his name.
   All on the plains of Mexico!

4. Oh, Santy Anna fought for gold,
   Hooray, Santy Anna!
   And the deeds he's done have oft been told.
   All on the plains of Mexico!

5. And Santy Anna fought for his life,
   Hooray, Santy Anna!
   But he gained his way in the terrible strife.
   All on the plains of Mexico!

6. Oh, Santy Anna's day is o'er,
   Hooray, Santy Anna!
   And Santy Anna will fight no more.
   All on the plains of Mexico!

7. I thought I heard the Old Man say
   Hooray, Santy Anna!
   He'd give us grog this very day.
   All on the plains of Mexico!

Jump Jim Crow

"Jim Crow" introduced the Negro style of dancing to the stage. It was the invention of Thomas Dartmouth ("Daddy") Rice, who got the idea for title, tune, and dance step while watching an old Negro stablehand do some tricky steps to his own humming. Cincinnati, Louisville, and Pittsburgh all claim its first performance. Its tremendous success insured the future of Negro songs as entertainment and started the minstrel vogue.

1. Come, lis-ten, all you gals and boys, I'm just from Tuck-y-
2. I____ went down to de riv____-er, I did-n't mean to

hoe; I'm gwine to sing a lit-tle song, My name's____ Jim____
stay, But there I see so man-y gals, I could-n't get a-

3. I'm a rorer on de fiddle,
   An' down in ole Virginny,
   Dey say I play de skientific,
   Like massa Pagganninny.
   Chorus

4. I cut so many munky shines,
   I dance de galloppade;
   An' w'en I done, I res' my head,
   On shubble, hoe or spade.
   Chorus

5. I met Miss Dina Scrub one day,
   I gib her sich a buss;
   An' den she turn an' slap my face,
   An' make a mighty fuss.
   Chorus

6. De udder gals dey 'gin to fight,
   I tel'd dem wait a bit;
   I'd hab dem all, jis one by one,
   As I tourt fit.
   Chorus

7. I wip de lion ob de west,
   I eat de alligator;
   I put more water in my mouf,
   Den boil ten load ob 'tator.
   Chorus

8. De way dey bake de hoe cake,
   Virginny nebber tire;
   Dey put de doe upon de foot,
   An' stick 'em in de fire.
   Chorus

CHORUS
Wheel about, and turn about,
And do jis so;
Eb'ry time I wheel about,
I jump Jim Crow.

Over There

The origin of this song is a mystery. It was published in 1844.

Dolefully

1. Oh! po - ta - toes they grow small O - ver there! Oh! po -
2. Oh! the can - dles they are small O - ver there! Oh! the

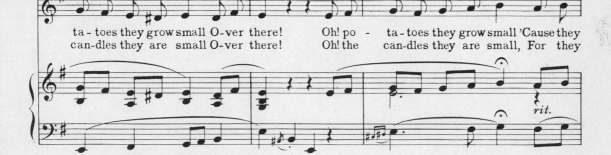

ta - toes they grow small O-ver there! Oh! po - ta-toes they grow small 'Cause they
can - dles they are small O-ver there! Oh! the can-dles they are small, For they

plant 'em in the fall, And then eats 'em tops and all O - ver there!
dips 'em lean and tall— And then burns 'em sticks and all O - ver there!

3. Oh! I wish I was a geese,
   All forlorn!
Oh! I wish I was a geese,
   All forlorn!
Oh! I wish I was a geese,
'Cause they lives and dies in peace,
And accumulates much grease
   Eating corn!

4. Oh! they had a clam pie
   Over there!
Oh! they had a clam pie
   Over there!
Oh! they had a clam pie,
And the crust was made of rye—
You must eat it, or must die,
   Over there!

The Ole Grey Goose

*The goose appears frequently in American animal songs
There are many versions of "The Ole Grey Goose," but
there is no clue to the authorship
of any of them.*

Oh! look-y whar? Look right o-ber yan-der.

Don't you see de Ole Grey Goose Smil-ing at de gan-der?

3. I ask Miss Dinah Rose one day
In de ole cart to ride.
She war, by gosh, so bery fat
I couldn't sit beside.
Chorus

4. When she was gittin' out de cart
Miss Dinah loose her shoe
And den I spied a great big hole
Right in her stocking through.
Chorus

5. Says I to her, "You Dinah Gal,
Only looky dar.
Dem heels are sticking out too far
To you I declar."
Chorus

6. Says she to me, "Now listen, Jo,
What are you about?
Dere's science in dem dar heels
And I want 'em to stick out."
Chorus

CHORUS
Oh! looky har. Oh! looky whar?
Look right ober yander.
Don't you see de Ole Grey Goose
Smiling at de gander?

Shuckin' of the Corn

Corn-shucking parties were important social gatherings. The shuckers worked busily and merrily, always on the lookout for the coveted red ear, for the lucky finder might kiss anyone of his, or her, choice— a custom that still holds.

1. I have a ship on the o - cean,_____ All lined with
2. The wind blows cold in__ Cai - ro,_____ The sun re -

sil - ver and gold._____ Be - fore I'd see my
fus - es to shine._____ Be - fore I'd see my

true love suf - fer, That ship should be an - chored and sold.
true love suf - fer, I'd work all the sum - mer time._____

Chorus

I'm a - go-in' to the shuck-in' of the corn,_____ I'm a - go-in' to the
shuck-in' of the corn,_____ A - shuck-in' of the corn and a-
blow-in' of the horn, I'm a - go in' to the shuck-in' of the corn._____

297

El-a-noy

A typical pioneer ballad—vigorous, optimistic, and imaginative.

Allegro
mf

c min   f min   g min

1. Way down___ up-on the Wa-bash, Sich___ land was nev-er
2. 'Twas here___ the Queen of She-ba came With Sol-o-mon of

non legato

c min   c min   g min   c min   g min   c min   g min

known,   If___ Ad-am had passed o-ver it, The soil he'd sure-ly
old,   With a don-key load of spic-es, Pome-gra-nates and fine

Ped.   Ped.   Ped.   Ped.   Ped.   Ped.

c min   g min   A♭   E♭

own;   He'd think it was the gar-den___ He'd play'd in when a
gold;   And when she saw this love-ly land Her heart was fill'd with

Ped.   Ped.   Ped.   Ped.   Ped.   Ped.   Ped.

298

boy, And straight pro-nounce it E - den In the state of El - a -
joy, Straight - way she said, "I'd like to be a queen in El - a -

noy. }
noy." } Then move your fam-'ly west-ward, Good health you will en -

joy, And rise to wealth and hon - or In the state of El - a - noy!

3. She's bounded by the Wabash,
   The Ohio, and the Lakes;
   She's crawfish in the marshes,
   The milk-sick and the shakes,
   But these are slight diversions,
   And take not from the joy
   Of living in this garden land,
   The state of El-a-noy.

   CHORUS
   Then move your fam'ly westward,
   Good health you will enjoy,
   And rise to wealth and honor
   In the state of El-a-noy!

Come, Come, Ye Saints

*In 1848 Brigham Young and a large body of Mormons, who called themselves "Latter Day Saints,"
set off on a long and dangerous journey to their new home in Salt Lake City. On the way, William
Clayton wrote the hymn "Come, Come, Ye Saints" for the Saints to sing, hoping to help them
forget their troubles. It has become the official Mormon hymn.*

Andante con moto

Words and Music by William Clayton

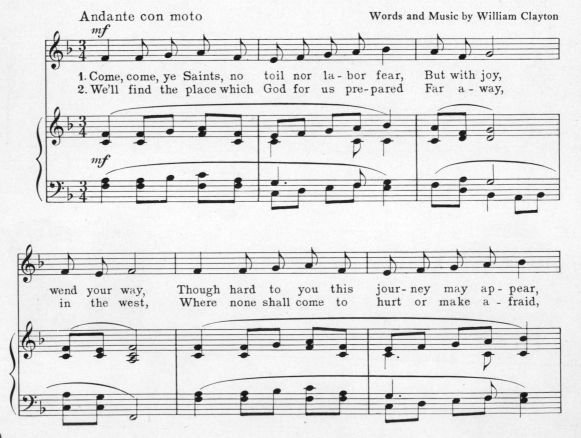

1. Come, come, ye Saints, no toil nor la-bor fear, But with joy,
2. We'll find the place which God for us pre-pared Far a-way,

wend your way, Though hard to you this jour-ney may ap-pear,
in the west, Where none shall come to hurt or make a-fraid,

Grace shall be as your day, 'Tis_ bet - ter far_ for
There the Saints will be blessed! We'll_ make the air_ with

us to strive_ Our use - less cares_ from us to drive; Do
mu - sic ring,_ Shout prais - es to_ our God and King! A -

this and joy your hearts will swell! All is well! All is well!
bove the rest each tongue will tell— All is well! All is well!

3. And should we die before our journey's through,
Happy day! All is well!
We then are free from toil and sorrow too;
With the just we shall dwell.
But if our lives are spared again
To see the Saints, their rest obtain,
O how we'll make this chorus swell—
All is well—all is well!

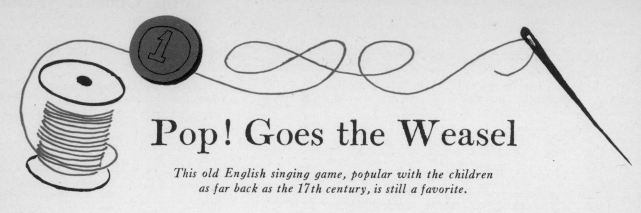

Pop! Goes the Weasel

*This old English singing game, popular with the children
as far back as the 17th century, is still a favorite.*

Allegro — with pep

1. A pen - ny for a spool___ of thread, A pen - ny for a nee - dle, That's the way the mon - ey goes, Pop! goes the wea - sel.

2. Po - ta - toes for an I - rish - man's taste, A doc - tor for the meas - les, A fid - dler al - ways for___ a dance, Pop! goes the wea - sel. Blood-

Pop! Goes the Weasel

All a-round the cob-bler's bench The mon-key chased the wea-sel, The
pud-ding for a Dutch-man's meal, A work-man for a chis-el, The

mon-key thought 'twas all in fun, Pop! goes the wea-sel.
tune that ev-'ry-bod-y sings Pop! goes the wea-sel.

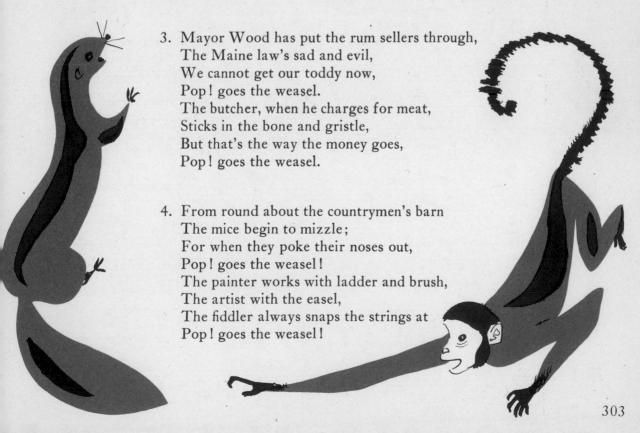

3. Mayor Wood has put the rum sellers through,
The Maine law's sad and evil,
We cannot get our toddy now,
Pop! goes the weasel.
The butcher, when he charges for meat,
Sticks in the bone and gristle,
But that's the way the money goes,
Pop! goes the weasel.

4. From round about the countrymen's barn
The mice begin to mizzle;
For when they poke their noses out,
Pop! goes the weasel!
The painter works with ladder and brush,
The artist with the easel,
The fiddler always snaps the strings at
Pop! goes the weasel!

Old Dan Tucker

"Old Dan Tucker," written as early as 1830, was first published in 1843.
It then became one of the most popular of all the minstrel songs.
It was also a favorite of play-party and square-dancing groups.

With plenty of "go"

Words and Music by Daniel Decatur Emmett

1. I came to town____ de ud-der night, I hear de noise, den
2. Old Dan-iel Tuck-er was a might-y man, He washed his face in a

saw de fight, De watch-man was a-run-nin' 'roun', Cry-in'
fry-ing pan,____ Combed his head wid a wag-on wheel, An'____

"Old Dan____ Tuck-er's come to town." } So git out de way,
died wid de tooth-ache in his heel.

Old Dan Tuck-er, Git out de way, Old Dan Tuck-er, Git out de way,

Old Dan Tuck-er, You're too late to come to sup-per.

3. Old Dan Tucker's back in town,
   Swingin' the ladies all aroun';
   First to the right and then to the left,
   An' then to the gal that he loves best.

4. Old Dan Tucker he got drunk,
   He fell in de fire an' he kicked up a chunk;
   De red hot coals got in his shoe
   An' whee-wee! how de ashes flew!

5. Tucker is a nice old man,
   He us'd to ride our darby ram,
   He sent him whizzin' down de hill;
   If he hadn't got up, he'd laid dar still.

305

Sacramento

The year 1849: Sacramento and the Gold Rush to California! There were two possible ways to reach the gold fields: one by ship around Cape Horn, the other by wagon train across the Great Plains.
Both were hazardous.

Words and Melody adapted and arranged by Joanna Colcord

1. A bul-ly ship and a bul-ly crew, Doo-da, doo-da! A
2. A-round Cape Horn in the month of snows Doo-da, doo-da! We

bul-ly mate and a cap-tain too, Doo-da, doo-da-day. Then
came to the land where the cock-tail flows, Doo-da, doo-da-day.

Chorus

blow ye winds, hi-oh, For Cal-i-for-ny-o! There's

plen-ty of gold, so I've been told, On the banks of the Sac-ra-men-to.

What Was Your Name in the States?

A strange medley of men were the thousands who joined the gold rush to California. Here was an opportunity for anyone, honest man or fugitive, to make a new life for himself.

Relaxed and easy tempo

Oh, what was your name in the States? Was it Thomp-son or John-son or Bates? Did you mur-der your wife And fly for your life? Say, what was your name in the States?

The Promised Land
BEFORE 1776

WE LEARN from the songs the people sang in the first century and a half of American history something of the grim spirit of religious rebellion which dominated the minds of the early colonists. From Virginia to New England in those early days the church was all-important. The colonists had emigrated because they were opposed to a firm order in England. But they created an order of their own which was just as bound up with the state as the old order which they had fled. In Massachusetts the church *was* the state, and no man could hold office or even vote unless he was a member of the church. Even in secular Virginia, the state frowned on Maypoles and theatres and work on the Sabbath day.

Perhaps, too, the severity of their early songs was a reflection of the barren, hardworking life which the people had to lead. It is true that some of the first accounts of America were glowing. Captain Arthur Barlowe, one of the first Englishmen to set foot in America, wrote: "The soil is the most plentiful, sweet, fruitful and wholesome of all the world; there are above fourteen several sweet smelling timber trees . . . they have those Oaks that we have, but far greater and better. Ourselves proved the soil and put some of our Peas in the ground, and in ten days they were fourteen inches high; they have also Beans very fair, of diverse colours and wonderful plenty; some growing naturally and some in their gardens, and so have they both wheat and oats." It sounded incredibly lush, almost like the "rocks and hills and brooks and vales" which flowed with milk and honey in the old hymn.

But nothing could have been more deluding than such early reports. The American colonists met with severe climates, unknown diseases, hunger, and Indian hostility. Half of the first colony in Jamestown died during that summer of 1607. In the cold of a New England winter, more than half of the first Pilgrim colonists were wiped out. Only a very strong motive could have made people endure the hardships of this new home, which in their early experience was so far from being a land of milk and honey. But they had that motive, the motive of rebellion. Our first colonists were rebels against an established order in the old land. They were dissenters in politics and dissenters in religion; first and foremost, dissenters in religion. And so they continued to come.

In the new land, however, there was also religious dissension. Settled by rebels, the colonies produced a breed of men who would not tolerate intolerance. Rebellion broke out against the dominating church state of Massachusetts. Roger Williams, who believed that the church and the state should be separate, was driven into exile and founded a colony of his own at Providence, Rhode Island. Anne Hutchinson, also exiled, was a founder of another colony at Portsmouth, Rhode Island. Other dissatisfied colonists went into Connecticut and New Hampshire and started their own settlements. It was no more possible for their fellow Americans to dominate the free-thinkers than it had been for their English forefathers. Religious revolts were sporadic, but they undermined the established order. And finally they culminated in the most widespread rebellion of all—the Great Awakening of the 1730's and '40's.

The Great Awakening was not a unified movement. But it occurred so spontaneously through the country that it had the effect of one, and it tore down the old traditions everywhere. Led by individual ministers—Jonathan Edwards, George Whitefield, the Tennents, and many others—the movement broke through all denominational lines. Its followers, who were called the "New Lights," held wildly emotional revival meetings and proclaimed their belief that men and women of all faiths could find salvation. They dissented from all authority, religious or civil. The conservatives feared them so much that they clapped their leaders into jail, and punished people for listening to them. But by the time the movement died down, it had accomplished its purpose: the hidebound rulings of the older church no longer had power over the minds and lives of men.

The religious music of those early days followed the course of religious dissension. For a time, church music was so limited by the narrow theological ideas of our forebears that it was barely music at all, and played a very unimportant part in the services. In place of the Latin music of the Church of England, the Puritans substituted psalms adapted from the Calvinist psalms of France and Holland. They were sung to tunes based on European secular folk music. The words were awkward—a literal adaptation of the Psalms.

The first book of church music used by the Pilgrims in this country was *The Ainsworth Psalter,* which they brought with them from Holland, where it had been printed in 1612. Only three of the Psalms from this book are generally known today: "Old Hundredth" and "Toulon," which are included here, and the famous battle song of the Huguenots, sometimes called the "Huguenot Marseillaise," which begins, "Confess Jehovah Thankfully" (Psalm 84).

Then in 1640 *The Bay Psalm Book* was published in Cambridge, Massachusetts, the first book printed in English-speaking North America. It was modeled on the English standard psalm book edited by Sternhold and Hopkins. The psalms were shorter and were sung to shorter and easier tunes. This was a first step toward the liberalization of church music. The early edition of *The Bay Psalm Book,* however, printed no music, and the congregations had to rely on their memories for the tunes. Since many of the congregation could not read and knew nothing about music, the psalms were read line by line ("lined out") and intoned ("set") by the deacon or a person appointed by him, and the congregation repeated line by line after him. This alternation resulted in a slow pace and a limping uncertain style which caused John Adams to describe the church music of the time as embodying "all the drawling quavering discord in the world." It was not until 1698, in the ninth edition of *The Bay Psalm Book,* that music was included, and then there were only thirteen tunes.

Psalm singing held its sway for a good century and a quarter, but during this time other and more liberal forms of music were being introduced in the church services. In England, Isaac Watts broke away from the established form and wrote hymns which were called "man-made" in contradistinction to the divine or literal renditions of the psalms. These man-made hymns were considered extremely daring, but Watts succeeded in establishing them as an accepted part of public worship. In America they were enormously popular. Many of them are still sung today. "O God, Our Help in Ages Past" and "When I Survey Thy Wondrous Cross" are perhaps the best known.

About the same time, considerable numbers of Germans and Moravians were migrating to this country, settling for the most part in Pennsylvania. They brought with them the extremely singable church music which had been popularized in Germany by Martin Luther. It was based on German folk music and included many examples of the man-made hymn. And even at this early date the Germans used carols in their church services. The Pilgrims and their followers, however, held the Puritan view regarding church celebrations and discouraged carol singing and all Christmas festivities.

In Georgia, John and Charles Wesley also wrote a number of man-made hymns. Unfortunately, they went to the German and Moravian music for settings for their hymns. The combination of English words and German music was not always a happy one, although many Wesley hymns are still popular today.

With the Great Awakening the folk hymn, which sprang from the people by the same process as the ballad or folk song, came into being. Actually, we have no record that folk hymns were widely sung until the 1770's, but there are many indications that they were in use much earlier. Again there is no proof that the tunes used here for the old hymns are the original ones, for their origins are obscure. In any case, these versions have been sung for many years and appear in this form in the earlier American song books.

By the time of the Great Awakening, the church was no longer dominant in America. The country had grown considerably and the colonies had become a financial success. In the South, the planters were reaping handsome profits from their tobacco and rice plantations, while in New England tradesmen sent shiploads of furs and lumber back to the old country. By the middle of the eighteenth century, the colonies were even threatening English shipping itself. We were building more than one hundred and fifty new ships a year, and were attracting skilled laborers from the English shipyards. Our venturesome crews largely took over the whale trade, and our ships plied down to the West Indies to buy sugar and molasses for rum, and across to Africa to use the American-made rum in the slave trade. Old English sea songs, undoubtedly picked up by our sailors in their cross-Atlantic voyages, and pirate songs too, became part of our experience. During England's wars with the French, Dutch, and Spanish, American merchant ships became privateers and took rich prizes from enemy cargoes. When the wars were over, it was inevitable that some of the privateers went on taking prizes, and their exploits were celebrated in the pirate songs of the day.

By the time of the Revolution, even—in fact, before it—the American colonists had developed a character of their own. America was already a melting pot amalgamating many strains. After the Puritan immigrations came the Cavalier immigrations, which in Maryland and the Carolinas founded colonies with a broader religious freedom, as expressed in the Catholic Toleration Act. Swedes and Dutch had settled here early. Now men and women from other countries came in waves of immigration—economic, political, and religious refugees. Vast numbers of Germans fled from native tyranny. Scotch-Irish, Irish, Welsh, French Huguenots, Swiss, Italians, and Portuguese Jews sought the new freedom of the colonies. They numbered only a tenth to a quarter of the whole population (the English-speaking colonists at that time constituting the balance), but they brought with them their own folklore, literature, and songs. And these made their mark, as the songs we now sing can testify: "Shule Agra," "All Through the Night," "Robin Adair," "Aupres de Ma Blonde," "Die Abendglocke," and many others. This mixture of culture, of peoples and of races, was the beginning of a great heritage, a heritage which has shaped the whole of American history.

Old Hundredth

This French tune from The Ainsworth Psalter *was in its early form a "gay, lively, jocund air."*
The slower form, used today, emerged from the 18th century.
The second stanza, by Thomas Ken, is known as the "Doxology."

Words of 2nd stanza by Thomas Ken   Music by Louis Bourgeois

With majesty

1. Shout to Je - ho - vah, all the earth; Serve ye Je - ho - vah with glad-nes; Be -
2. Praise God from Whom all bless-ings flow, Praise Him all crea-tures here be - low, Praise

Octaves ad lib.

fore Him come with sing - ing mirth; Know that Je - ho - vah He God is.
Him a - bove, ye heav'n-ly host; Praise Fa - ther, Son, and Ho - ly Ghost.

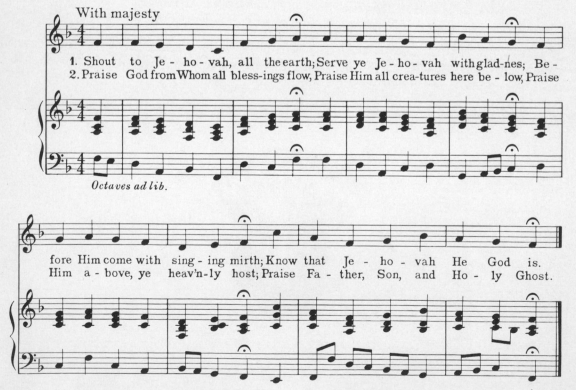

Pilgrims' Melody

Also from The Ainsworth Psalter, *this is an old French tune attributed to Louis Bourgeois. Originally of five lines, it is now commonly reduced to four (the third is the line omitted). This modified version is called "Toulon."*

Psalm 8

Allegro

Our Is - ra - el may say and that tru - ly,

If that the Lord had not our cause main-tain'd, If that the Lord had

not our right sus - tain'd When all the world a - gainst us fu - rious - ly

Made their up - roars and said we all should die.

313

York

"York" is found in the ninth edition of The Bay Psalm Book, *the first edition of this book to include tunes. It was originally called "The Stilt" because of the melodic imitation in the first and third phrases of the motion of the legs walking on stilts.*

Psalm 66

Melody arranged by T. Ravenscroft

Ye men of earth in God re-joice, With praise set forth His name;

Ex - tol His might with heart and voice, Give glo-ry to the same.

Windsor

This is another of the thirteen tunes from the ninth edition of The Bay Psalm Book. *In the* Scottish Psalter *of 1635 it is called "Dundie." In modern hymnals it appears under the name "Windsor."*

Psalm 108

Melody arranged by T. Ravenscroft

Andante con moto

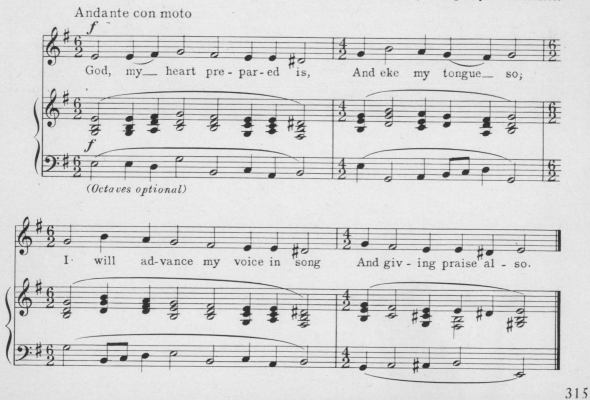

God, my____ heart pre-par-ed is, And eke my tongue____ so;

(Octaves optional)

I will ad-vance my voice in song And giv-ing praise al - so.

Barb'ry Ellen

The story of Barb'ry Ellen is popular in innumerable versions through all parts of America: in the Kentucky mountains, in the New England states, in Mississippi, in Georgia and Nebraska. Ninety-eight different versions have been found in Virginia alone. This Scottish version, according to Miss Linscott, in her Folk Songs of Old New England, *was sung by the descendants of one Ralph Ellwood, who came in September 1635 from England in the ship "True Love" to Salem.*

Very freely

1. In Lim-'rick cit-y he was brought up, And Dub-lin was his sta-tion; He
2. When he took sick and ve-ry ill, He sent for Bar-b'ry El-len. But

fell in love with a nice young girl, Her name was Bar-b'ry El-len.
when she came, was all she said, "Young man, I think you're dy-in'."

3. "Dying. Oh, no! That ne'er can be
   One kiss from you would cure me."
   "One kiss from me you ne'er shall get
   If your very heart was breaking!"

4. He died and was buried in churchyard near,
   And she was buried in the choir.
   And out of his grave grew a red, red rose,
   And out of hers grew a brier.

5. They grew and they grew to the steeple top;
   They could not grow any higher,
   And then they twined in a true lover's knot
   The red rose and the brier.

From E. H. Linscott: *Folk Songs of Old New England.*
Copyright 1939 by The Macmillan Co., and used with their permission.

Go from My Window

The tune is an old one and appears in Queen Elizabeth's Virginal Book. It is very like that of Ophelia's song—"And how should I your true love know?" The words used here are traditional.

Go from my win-dow, my love, my love, Go from my win-dow, my dear; For the wind is in the west, And the cuck-oo in his nest, And you can't have a lodg-ing here.

317

See My Wagon, It's Full-Laden

('K HEB MIJN WAGEN VOLGELADEN)

A gay seaman's song, popular among the Dutch when New York was still New Amsterdam.

Translation by Freda Morrill Abrams

1. 'k Heb mijn wag-en vol-ge-la-den Vol met ou-de wij-ven, Toen ze op de mar(re)-kt kwa-men Be-gon-nen

1. See my wag-on, it's well la-den, Now old wives it's hold-ing. When to mar-ket they are com-ing, They are

zij te kij - ven; / quar- rel-ing and scold-ing. Nu - neem ik van mijn le - vens da - gen / Nev - er a - gain I'll take, for my part,

Geen ou - de wij - ven op mijn wa - gen, / An - y old wives up - on my horse - cart. Hop, paard - je, hop! / Hup, hor - sey, hup!

2. See my wagon, it's well laden,
   With old men we're trotting.
   When to market they're coming,
   They're scheming and they're plotting.

   Never again I'll take, for my part,
   Any old men upon my horse-cart.
   Hup, horsey, hup!

3. See my wagon, 'gain it's laden,
   Now young girls it's bringing.
   When to market they're coming,
   Like songbirds they are singing!

   Now all my life I'll take, for my part,
   Young maidens always on my horse-cart.
   Hup, horsey, hup!

Little Hypocrite

(HET KWEZELKEN)

*A charming folk song with the ever-popular
courtship theme. Kwezelken, probably derived
from the same root as the German* Keusch, *meaning "chaste," has come to mean in
modern Dutch "little hypocrite."*

English version by Freda Morrill Abrams

1. "Zeg, kwe-zel-ken, wil-de gy dan-sen? Ik zal u ge-ven een
1. "Say, Kwe-zel-ken, will you go danc-ing? An egg I'll give to

ei!" "Wel neen ik," zei dat kwe-zel-ken, "Van
you!" "Oh no, no," said the Kwe-zel-ken, "For

dan-sen ben ik vrij 'k En kan niet dan-sen, 'k En
danc-ing I do not do. I don't go danc-ing, I

mag   niet   dan - sen,   Dan - sen is in onz'
can't go   danc - ing,   Danc - ing we're not al -

re gel niet, Be - gijn - tjes en kwe - zel - kens dan - sen niet?"
lowed to do, Be - quin - es* and Kwe - zels can't dance with you?"

*nuns

2. "Say, Kwezelken, will you go dancing?
    I shall give you a cow."
    "Oh no, no," said the Kwezelken,
    "To dance I don't know how.
    Chorus

3. "Say, Kwezelken, will you go dancing?
    A horse I'll give to you."
    "Oh no, no," said the Kwezelken,
    "I wish no dancing to do.
    Chorus

4. "Say, Kwezelken, will you go dancing?
    I shall give you a man !"
    "Yes, surely," said the Kwezelken,
    "I'll dance as well as I can.

FINAL CHORUS
"I can go dancing, I WILL go dancing,
Dancing is all right to do
And I will surely dance with you."

The Evening Bells

(DIE ABENDGLOCKE)

Rounds, popular in Europe since the 17th century, were undoubtedly sung by the early colonists, and frequently then, as now, in their original language.

Andante

O wie wohl ist mir am A - bend, mir am A - bend, Wenn zur

Ruh' die Glock - e lau - ten, Glock - e lau - ten, Bim, bam,

Voices 2 and 3 continue until each has sung

bim, bam, bim, bam.

all of the melody

Oh, how lovely is the evening, is the evening,
When to rest the bells are ringing, bells are ringing,
Bim, bam, bim, bam, bim, bam.

A Mighty Fortress Is Our God

(EIN' FESTE BURG)

Martin Luther's famous hymn, published in 1535, has been used as a battle cry throughout the centuries since. It was the battle cry of the Reformation, and recently, in 1942, most dramatically, the Norwegians sang it when defying the Nazi order to close the ancient Trondheim Cathedral.

Translation by F. H. Hedge

Music by Martin Luther

Ein' fes - te Burg ist un - ser Gott, Ein' gu - te
Er hilft uns frei_ aus al - ler Noth, Die uns hat

Wehr und Waf - -fen. Der alt'_ bö - se Feind, Mit
jetzt be - trof - -fen

Ernst er's jetzt meint: Gross Macht und viel List, Ein'
grau- sam Rüf- tung ist, Auf Erd' ist nicht sein glei- - chen.

1. A mighty fortress is our God,
   A bulwark never failing;
   Our helper He, amid the flood
   Of mortal ills prevailing.
   For still our ancient foe
   Doth seek to work us woe;
   His craft and pow'r are great,
   And arm'd with cruel hate,
   On earth is not his equal.

2. Did we in our own strength confide,
   Our striving would be losing;
   Were not the right man on our side,
   The man of God's own choosing.
   Dost ask who that may be?
   Christ Jesus, it is He;
   Lord Sabaoth His Name,
   From age to age the same,
   And He must win the battle.

Joseph, Dearest Joseph

(JOSEPH, LIEBER JOSEPH)

A charming German Christmas dialogue song which dates from the 14th century.

Translation by Freda Morrill Abrams

Joseph, lie-ber Jo-seph mein, Hilf mir wie-gen mein
Joseph dear-est, Jo-seph sweet, Help me rock my

Kin-de-lein! Gott, der wird dein Loh-ner sein In Him-mel-
babe to sleep, Bless-ings for you God will keep In Heav'n a-

reich der Jung-frau Sohn Ma-ri-a. Er ist er-
bove, O Son of Vir-gin Ma-ry. O He is

schie-nen am heu-ti-gen Tag, Am heu-ti-gen Tag in Is-ra-el,
come to us this ver-y day, On this ver-y day in Is-ra-el,

Der Ma - ri - a ver - kün - digt - ist durch Ga - bri - el. Ei - a,
And to Ma - ry 'twas first an - nounced by Ga - bri - el. Hal - le

Ei - a. Je - sum Christ hat uns ge - boren Ma - ri - a.
lu - ja! Un - to us is Je - sus born of Ma - ry.

Er ist er - schie - nen am heu - ti - gen Tag, Am heu - ti - gen Tag in
O He is come to us this ver - y day, On this ver - y day in

Is - ra - el, Von Ma - ri - a ist Heil er - spros - sen in al - le Welt.
Is - ra - el, Now from Ma - ry sal - va - tion comes for all the world.

327

In Dulci Jubilo

The Moravians brought with them to America a great tradition of music: they used it in worship, at work, and at play. Each day a time was set aside for communal singing, and services called "love feasts" were held on Saturdays and on special occasions. It is said that at a "love feast" held on September 14, 1745, the German hymn "In Dulci Jubilo" was sung simultaneously and spontaneously in thirteen languages, including Bohemian, Dutch, English, French, German, Irish, Mohawk, Mohican, Swedish, Welsh, and Wendish.

Con moto

Translation by Percy Dearmer

1. In dul - ci ju - bi - lo_____ Now sing with
2. O Je - su par - vu - le,_____ For thee I

hearts a - glow!_____ Our de - light and pleas -
long al - way;_____ Com - fort my heart's blind -

ure   Lies   in   prae - sip - i - o._____   Like   sun - shine
ness,   O   pu - er   op - ti - me_____   With   all   thy

is   our   treas - ure,   Ma - tris   in   grem - i - o._____
lov - ing   kind - ness,   O   prin - ceps   glo - ri - ae._____

Al - pha   es   et   O!_____   Al - pha   es   et   O!
Tra - he   me   post   te!_____   Tra - he   me   post   te!

329

Spanish Ladies

A spirited old English sea song, popular with American as well as with English sailors.

1. Fare - well and a - dieu to____ you, Span - ish
Chorus We'll____ rant and we'll roar like____ true Brit - ish

la - dies, Fare - well and a - dieu to you, la - dies of
sail - ors, We'll rant and we'll roar____ all on the high

Spain; For we've re-ceived or-ders for to sail for old
seas Un - til we strike sound - ings in the chan-nel of old

Eng - land, But we hope in a short time to see you a - gain.
Eng - land, From U - shant to Scil - ly is thir - ty - five leagues.

2. We hove our ship to, with the wind from sou'west, boys,
   We hove our ship to, deep soundings to take;
   'Twas forty-five fathoms, with a white sandy bottom,
   So we squared our main yard and up channel did make.
   Chorus

3. The first land we sighted was called the Dodman;
   Next, Rame Head off Plymouth, off Portsmouth the Wight;
   We sailed by Beachy, by Fairlight and Dover,
   And then we bore up for the South Foreland light.
   Chorus

4. Then the signal was made for the grand fleet to anchor,
   And all in the Downs that night for to lie;
   Let go your shank painter, let go your cat stopper!
   Haul up your clewgarnets, let tacks and sheets fly!
   Chorus

5. Now let ev'ry man drink off his full bumper,
   And let ev'ry man drink off his full glass;
   We'll drink and be jolly and drown melancholy,
   And here's to the health of each true-hearted lass.
   Chorus

Captain Kidd

An old ballad which tells of the wicked deeds of a famous pirate, William Kidd (known as Robert in the ballad), who was active in American waters in the 17th century. Kidd was tried and hung for "murther and piracy" in London in 1701. This most popular of our bad-man ballads was written at the time of the trial.

1. Oh! My name was Rob-ert Kidd, as I sailed, as I sailed,
2. Oh! I mur-dered Wil-liam Moore, as I sailed, as I sailed,

Oh, my name was Rob-ert Kidd, as I sailed,
Oh, I mur-dered Wil-liam Moore, as I sailed,

My name was Rob-ert Kidd, God's
I mur-dered Wil-liam Moore and

laws I did for- bid, And most wick- ed - ly I did, as I
left him in his gore, Not___ man - y leagues from shore, as I

Broader

sailed, as I sailed, {And most wick-ed - ly I did, as I sailed.
{Not__ man - y leagues from shore, as I sailed.

3. Oh! I steered from sound to sound as I sailed, as I sailed,
   Oh, I steered from sound to sound as I sailed,
   I steered from sound to sound, and many ships I found,
   And most of them I burned, as I sailed, as I sailed,
   And most of them I burned as I sailed.

4. Oh! I'd ninety bars of gold, as I sailed, as I sailed,
   Oh, I'd ninety bars of gold, as I sailed,
   I'd ninety bars of gold, and dollars manifold,
   With riches uncontrolled, as I sailed, as I sailed,
   With riches uncontrolled, as I sailed.

5. Then fourteen ships I saw, as I sailed, as I sailed,
   Then fourteen ships I saw, as I sailed,
   Then fourteen ships I saw, and brave men they were,
   Ah! they were too much for me, as I sailed, as I sailed,
   Ah! they were too much for me, as I sailed.

6. Oh! Take warning now by me, for I must die, I must die,
   Oh, take warning now by me, for I must die,
   Take warning now by me, and shun bad company,
   Lest you come to hell with me, for I must die, I must die,
   Lest you come to hell with me, for I must die.

O God, Our Help in Ages Past

Words by Isaac Watts

Music by William Croft

Maestoso

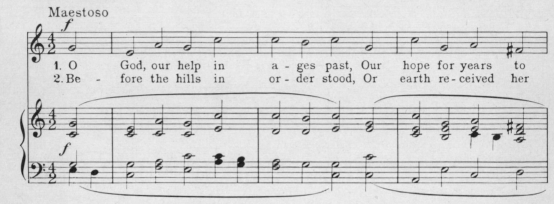

1. O God, our help in a-ges past, Our hope for years to
2. Be - fore the hills in or - der stood, Or earth re-ceived her

come, Our shel-ter from the storm-y blast, And our e-ter-nal home.
frame, From ev-er-last-ing Thou art God, To end-less years the same.

3. A thousand ages in Thy sight
   Are like an evening gone;
   Short as the watch that ends the night
   Before the rising sun.

4. O God, our help in ages past,
   Our hope for years to come,
   Be Thou our Guide while life shall last,
   And our eternal home.

334

Jesus, Lover of My Soul

John Wesley's earliest Collection of Psalms and Hymns, including original hymns by the Wesley brothers, was published in South Carolina in 1737 by Louis Timothy, Benjamin Franklin's partner. Charles Wesley wrote more than 6,000 hymns, one of them this universal favorite.

Words by Charles Wesley   Music by Simeon B. Marsh

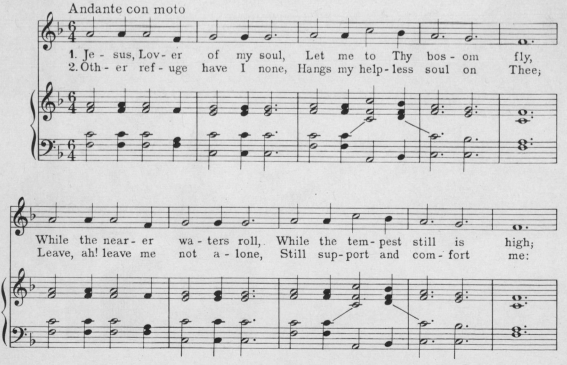

1. Je - sus, Lov - er of my soul, Let me to Thy bos - om fly,
2. Oth - er ref - uge have I none, Hangs my help - less soul on Thee;

While the near - er wa - ters roll, While the tem - pest still is high;
Leave, ah! leave me not a - lone, Still sup - port and com - fort me:

Hide me, O my Sav-iour, hide, Till the storm of life be past;
All my trust on Thee is stayed; All my help from Thee I bring;

Safe in-to the ha-ven guide, O re-ceive my soul at last.
Cov-er my de-fense-less head With the shad-ow of Thy wing.

3. Plenteous grace with Thee is found,
Grace to cleanse from every sin;
Let the healing streams abound,
Make and keep me pure within:
Thou of life the fountain art,
Freely let me take of Thee;
Spring Thou up within my heart,
Rise to all eternity. Amen.

All Through the Night

The ancient Welsh folk song, "Ar Hyd y Nos," was formerly sung to an English setting,
"Here beneath a willow weepeth poor Mary Ann." It is best known outside Wales
today by the title "All Through the Night."

Words by (Sir) Harold Boulton

1. Sleep, my child, and peace at-tend thee All through the night;
2. While the moon her watch is keep-ing All through the night;

Guard-ian an-gels God will send thee, All through the night.
While the wea-ry world is sleep-ing, All through the night.

Soft the drow-sy hours are creep-ing, Hill and vale in slum-ber sleep-ing,
O'er thy spir-it gent-ly steal-ing, Vi-sions of de-light re-veal-ing,

I my lov-ing vig-il keep-ing, All through the night.
Breathes a pure and ho-ly feel-ing, All through the night.

Reprinted by permission of J. B. Cramer & Co., Ltd., London, England.

We're Singing Our Praises

(WILT HEDEN NU TREDEN)

A song of praise written in 1597 to celebrate a Dutch victory. Sung to the words "We gather together to ask the Lord's blessing," it has become the accepted song of praise in America for Thanksgiving Day.

Translation by Freda Morrill Abrams

From Valerius—"Gedenck-Glanck"

With movement

Wilt he - den nu tre - den voor God____ den
Now sing - ing we're bring - ing our prais - es be -

Heere, Hem bo - ven al lo - ven van her - ten
fore Him, God prais - ing, we're rais - ing our voic - es on

seer, End' ma - ken groot zijns lie - ven na - mens
high. Our Lord's name we hon - or, we ev - er ex -

ee - re, Die daar nu on - sen vij - an slaat ter - neer.
tol Him, And we shall con - quer ev - il with God our al - ly.

English version by Dr. Theodore Baker

1. We gather together to ask the Lord's blessing;
He chastens and hastens His will to make known.
The wicked oppressing will cease from distressing,
Sing praises to His name, He forgets not His own.

2. Beside us to guide us, our God with us joining,
Ordaining, maintaining His Kingdom divine,
So from the beginning the fight we were winning;
Thou, Lord, wast at our side, the glory be Thine.

3. We all do extol Thee, Thou Leader in battle,
And pray that Thou still our Defender wilt be.
Let Thy congregation escape tribulation;
Thy name be ever praised! O Lord, make us free!

Auprès de Ma Blonde
(NEAR TO MY FAIR ONE)

"Auprès de Ma Blonde" was originally a children's song. Later, in the war between France and Holland in the 17th century, it became a favorite marching song of the French soldiers.

Translation by Freda Morrill Abrams

1. Dans le jar-din d'mon pèr-e Les li-lacs sont fleu-ris___ Dans
1. Oh, in my fa-ther's gar-den The li-lacs are in bloom,___ Oh,

le jar-din d'mon pèr-e Les li-lacs sont fleu-ris.___ Tous
in my fa-ther's gar-den The li-lacs are in bloom,___ And

les ois-eaux du mon-de y vien-nent fair' leur nid.___
all the birds are sing-ing, To make their nests they come.___

From *Work and Sing*, copyright 1948 by Cooperative Recreation Service, Delaware, Ohio.

Refrain

Au - près de ma blon - de   Qu'il fait bon, fait bon, fait bon,
Near to___ my fair one,   Oh, it's good, it's good, it's good,

Au - près de ma blon - de   Qu'il fait bon dor - mir!___
Near to___ my fair one,   Oh, it's good to be!___

2. The turtle-dove and quail
   And partridge bright and gay,
   The turtle-dove and quail
   And partridge bright and gay,
   And my white dove is singing,
   She's singing night and day.
   Chorus

3. She's singing for the maidens,
   For maids with husbands none,
   She's singing for the maidens,
   For maids with husbands none,
   It's not for me she's singing,
   For I've a handsome one.
   Chorus

4. But he is now in Holland,
   A prisoner is he;
   But he is now in Holland,
   A prisoner is he;
   "What would you give, my fine girl,
   To have him back with thee?"
   Chorus

5. Oh, I would give Versailles,
   Paris and St. Denis,
   Oh, I would give Versailles,
   Paris and St. Denis,
   The towers of Nôtre Dame
   And the bells of my country.
   Chorus

341

Robin Adair

*A Gaelic air claimed by both Scotland and Ireland.
A rhythmical figure called the "Scotch Snap"* first
appears in the song in the early 19th century.*

Andante con moto

Words by Caroline Keppel

1. What's this dull town to me? Ro-bin's not near.
2. What made th'as-sem-bly shine? Ro-bin A-dair.

What was't I wish'd to see, What wish'd to hear?
What made the ball so fine? Ro-bin was there.

342

Where's all the joy and mirth Made this town a heav'n on earth?
What when the play was o'er, What made my heart so sore?

Oh, they're all fled with thee, Ro - bin A - dair.
Oh, it was part - ing with Ro - bin A - dair.

3. But now thou'rt cold to me,
Robin Adair,
But now thou'rt cold to me,
Robin Adair,
Yet he I lov'd so well
Still in my heart shall dwell.
Oh, I can ne'er forget
Robin Adair.

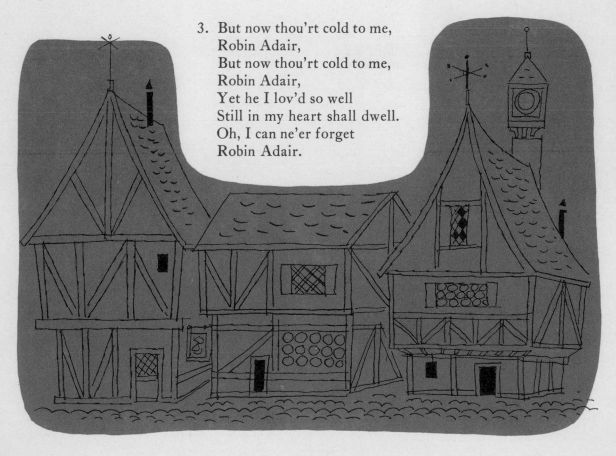

343

Shule Agra

A 17th-century Irish song of great beauty.

Words by A. P. Graves

1. His hair was black, his eye was blue, His arm was stout, his word was true. I wish in my heart I was with you, Go thee, thu Mavourneen slaun! *

2. I sold my rock, I sold my reel; When my flax was spun, I sold my wheel, To buy my love a sword of steel,

Chorus

Shule, shule, shule a gra! ‡ Only death can

344

From *Songs of the Four Nations* by permission of J. B. Cramer & Co., Ltd., London, England.

ease my woe, Since the lad of my heart from me did go, Go_ thee _ thu, Ma-

vour-neen slaun!

1st & 2d times

3d time

3. I'll dye my petticoat, I'll dye it red,
   And round the world I'll beg my bread,
   Till I find my love alive or dead.
   Go thee, thu Mavourneen slaun.
   Chorus

4. King James was routed in the fray;
   The "wild-geese" went with him away,
   My boy went too, that dreary day.
   Go thee, thu Mavourneen slaun.
   Chorus

*Farewell, my darling   †Come, come, my love

Malbrouck

The English general, the Duke of Marlborough, has become a legendary figure through the satirical song written after his victory at the battle of Malplaquet in 1709. In this song he appears under the shortened name of "Malbrouck." Percy Scholes says that the name "Malbrouck" appears also in the early literature of France in the Chansons de Gestes. Many jingles have been set to the tune in America: "For he's a jolly good fellow," "We won't go home till morning," "The bear went over the mountain." The original "Malbrouck," however, is still a popular song.

Translation by Freda Morrill Abrams

1. Mal - brouck s'en va - t'en guer - re, Mi - ron - ton, mi - ron - ton, mi - ron -
1. Mal - brouck has gone to bat - tle, Mi - ron - ton, mi - ron - ton, mi - ron -

tai - ne, Mal-brouck s'en va - t'en guer - re, Ne sait quand re - vien - dra!___
tai - ne, Mal-brouck has gone to bat - tle, Who knows when he'll re - turn!___

Ne sait quand re - vien - dra!___ Ne sait quand re - vien - dra!___
Who knows when he'll re - turn!___ Who knows when he'll re - turn!___

2. He won't come home till Easter,
   Mi-ron-ton, mi-ron-ton, mi-ron-tai-ne;
   He won't come home till Easter
   Or else at Trinity. Or else at Trinity. Or else at Trinity.*

3. But Trinity is over,
   Mir-ron-ton, mi-ron-ton, mi-ron-tai-ne;
   And where, O where, is he? *(3 times)*

4. His wife climbs to her tower, mi-ron-ton . . .
   To see what she can see. *(3 times)*

5. She sees her page approaching, mi-ron-ton . . .
   In black array is he. *(3 times)*

6. "O page, O page, do tell me, mi-ron-ton . . .
   What news, what news!" cried she. *(3 times)*

7. "At the news which I must bring you, mi-ron-ton . . .
   You'll weep most mournfully. *(3 times)*

8. "Madame, he fell in battle, mi-ron-ton . . .
   He was wounded mortally. *(3 times)*

9. "Cold in the grave they laid him, mi-ron-ton . . .
   His soldiers, one, two, three. *(3 times)*

10. "The first two bore his armor, mi-ron-ton . .
    And shield with dignity. *(3 times)*

11. "The third his sword was holding, mi-ron-ton . . .
    For everyone to see. *(3 times)*

12. "All 'round his tomb was planted, mi-ron-ton . . .
    Most fragrant rosemary. *(3 times)*

13. "A nightingale was singing, mi-ron-ton . . .
    Above us blithe and free. *(3 times)*

14. "We saw his soul then soaring, mi-ron-ton . . .
    Above the laurel tree. *(3 times)*

15. "In memory of our hero, mi-ron-ton . . .
    We all bowed solemnly. *(3 times)*

16. "Then sang of Malbrouck's glory, mi-ron-ton . . .
    And every victory. *(3 times)*

17. "Then all went home for dinner, mi-ron-ton . . .
    When done with eulogy. *(3 times)*

18. "And now my story's over, mi-ron-ton . . .
    It's plenty, you'll agree." *(3 times)*

*The Sunday next after Pentecost.

Come, Saints and Sinners

A religious ballad which, like secular ballads, tells a story, but a story of religious experience, of exhortation, and of union of man with God. These ballads, telling of personal experiences, were sung by individuals rather than by groups.

Allegro moderato

Transcribed by George Pullen Jackson

1. Come, saints and sin - ners, hear me tell the won - ders of Im-
2. When Je - sus from His throne on high Be - held my soul in

From George Pullen Jackson: *Spiritual Folk Songs of Early America*, published by J. J. Augustin, Publisher, New York. Used by permission.

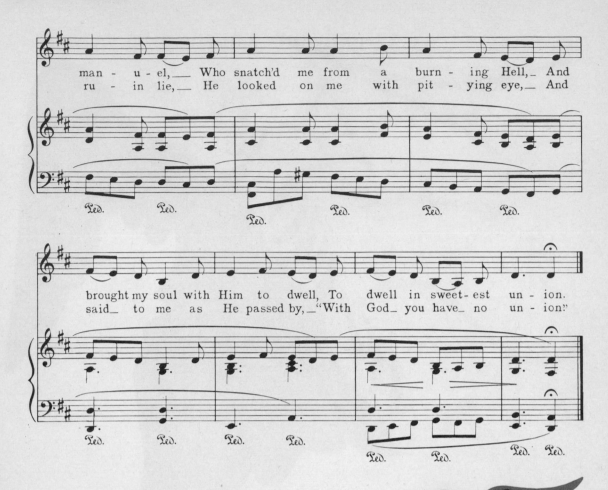

man - u - el,___ Who snatch'd me from a burn - ing Hell,___ And
ru - in lie,___ He looked on me with pit - ying eye,___ And

brought my soul with Him to dwell, To dwell in sweet - est un - ion.
said___ to me as He passed by,___ "With God___ you have___ no un - ion."

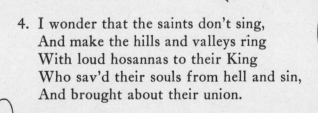

3. But when depressed and lost in sin,
My dear Redeemer took me in,
And with His blood He wash'd me clean,
And O what seasons I have seen!
Since first I felt this union.

4. I wonder that the saints don't sing,
And make the hills and valleys ring
With loud hosannas to their King
Who sav'd their souls from hell and sin,
And brought about their union.

5. Come, heaven and earth, unite your lays,
And give Jehovah-Jesus praise,
And thou, my soul, look up and gaze.
He bleeds, He dies, thy debt He pays
To give thee heavenly union.

Wondrous Love

*One of the most beautiful of the folk hymns. The stanzaic form
is that of the "Captain Kidd" ballad, which has been widely sung and parodied since the 18th century.*

Words by Rev. Alex Means **Transcribed by George Pullen Jackson**

1. What won-drous love is this, O my soul, O my soul! What
   won-drous love is this! O my soul! What won-drous love is
   this! That caused the Lord of bliss To bear the dread-ful curse for my
   soul, for my soul! To bear the dread-ful curse for my soul!

2. When I was sink-ing down, sink-ing down, sink-ing down, When
   I was sink-ing down, sink-ing down, When I was sink-ing
   down be-neath God's right-eous frown Christ laid a-side His crown for my
   soul, for my soul! Christ laid a-side His crown for my soul!

From George Pullen Jackson: *Spiritual Folk Songs of Early America,*
published by J. J. Augustin, Publisher, New York. Used by permission.

How Firm a Foundation

A famous folk hymn, still found in many of our modern hymnals.

Transcribed by George Pullen Jackson

1. How firm a foun-da-tion ye saints of the Lord, Is laid for your faith in His ex-cel-lent
2. Fear not, I am with thee, O be not dis-mayed, I, I am thy God, and will give thee

From George Pullen Jackson: *Down East Spirituals and Others*, published by J. J. Augustin, Publisher, New York. Used by permission.

word! What more can He say than to you He hath
aid; I'll strength-en thee, help thee, and cause thee to

said, You__ who un-to Je - sus for ref - uge have fled?
stand, Up - held by My right - eous, om - ni - po - tent hand.

3. The soul that on Jesus doth lean for repose,
   I will not, I will not desert to his foes;
   That soul, though all hell should endeavor to shake,
   I'll never, no never, no never forsake.

Greenfields

A secular English folk tune, "Farewell, Ye Green Fields and Sweet Groves," probably gave birth—according to George Pullen Jackson—to the religious song "Greenfields." This folk hymn, found in every old Southern song book, is said to have been a favorite song of Abraham Lincoln.

Andante con moto

Transcribed by George Pullen Jackson

1. How te-dious and taste-less the hours, When Je-sus no lon-ger I see; Sweet pros-pects, sweet birds and sweet flow'rs Have all lost their sweet-ness to me. The mid-sum-mer sun shines but dim, The fields strive in vain to look gay; But when I am hap-py in Him, De-cem-ber's as pleas-ant as May.

2. His name yields the rich-est per-fume, And sweet-er than mu-sic His voice; His pres-ence dis-per-ses my gloom, And makes all with-in me re-joice. I should, were He al-ways thus nigh, Have noth-ing to wish or to fear; No mor-tal as hap-py as I, My sum-mer would last all the year.

354

From George Pullen Jackson: *Spiritual Folk Songs of Early America*, published by J. J. Augustin, Publisher, New York. Used by permission.

INDEX OF FIRST LINES

355

INDEX OF TITLES

358

ABOUT THE CONTRIBUTORS

THE EDITORS

MARGARET BRADFORD BONI says of herself: "I was born in Birmingham, Alabama, and lived in Tallahassee, Florida, from the age of one until I finished college—Florida State College. Studied music in Germany for a year, then studied at the Institute of Musical Art (now the Juilliard School of Music). Decided to go into school music and worked with Hollis Dann, state supervisor of music in Pennsylvania, for my supervisor's degree.

I taught music in the public schools in Factoryville, Pennsylvania, at the Brearley School in New York City, and at the City and Country School where I now am. I have written six books of material for the recorder and edited *The Fireside Book of Folk Songs* and *Keep Singing, Keep Humming,* a collection of songs for children. I have also given recorder courses in the Department of General Education, New York University.

ANNE BROOKS is that rare creature, a native-born and -bred New Yorker. She attended City and Country and Lincoln Schools in that city, took a brief business course, and at seventeen was in the publishing business, performing such literary jobs as running a switchboard, typing labels, and sealing thousands of envelopes. She was an assistant editor when she left to do free-lance writing, and the same firm, William Morrow and Company, published her two novels, *Kingdom on Earth* and *Hang My Heart.* During the war Miss Brooks worked for the OWI, writing radio news shows, and while there married Jerome D. Ross. They have two children, and she combines the role of wife and mother with occasional editorial assignments.

THE ARRANGER

NORMAN LLOYD is a member of the faculty of the Juilliard School of Music. His recent compositions include the words and music for a choral ballet, "REST-LESS LAND"; music for the documentary film "COLONIAL WILLIAMSBURG"; and several ballets for José Limón. Mr. Lloyd has lectured extensively on the subject of American music and brings to this book his conviction that the American listener, performer, or composer should have a knowledge of his cultural heritage as expressed in our popular songs.

THE ARTIST

AURELIUS BATTAGLIA began his art career at the age of five, when he drew a picture of a chicken for his mother. He went on to attend the Corcoran School of Art in Washington, his home city. Then followed illustrating for newspapers and magazines and painting murals for children's rooms. Besides doing character development for the Walt Disney Studio, he taught art there. During World War II he planned educational films for the Navy. Mr. Battaglia now lives in New Jersey with his wife and small daughter, and devotes his time to book illustration.